LAUREL

FATHERS PLAYING CATCH WITH SONS

FATHERS PLAYING CATCH WITH SONS

Essays on Sport [Mostly Baseball]

Donald Hall

LAUREL

A LAUREL BOOK
Published by
Dell Publishing Co., Inc.
1 Dag Hammarskjold Plaza
New York, New York 10017

Many of the essays collected here appeared in somewhat different
form in the following books, journals, and magazines, to which
the author and publisher extend their thanks: "Fathers Playing Catch
with Sons" in *Playboy* and in *Playing Around*, ed. Gerard McCauley
(Little, Brown, & Co.); "Baseball and the Meaning of Life" in
National Review, (© by National Review, Inc., 150 East 35th Street,
New York, NY 10016, reprinted by permission); "O Fenway Park"
in *Ford Times* (under the title "Fenway Park: Age Cannot Wither
Her," April 1977, reprinted courtesy of Ford Times); "The Poet's
Game" in *Inside Sports;* "The Necessary Shape of the Old-Timers
Game" in the program of the 1984 Cracker Jack Old Timers Baseball
Classic (forthcoming; printed by permission); "The Country of
Baseball" in *Dock Ellis in the Country of Baseball*, by Donald Hall
and Dock Ellis (Coward, McCann & Geoghegan, Inc., 1974);
"Proseball" as separate reviews in *The Times Literary Supplement*
(reprinted by permission), *The New York Times Book Review*
(Copyright © 1976, 1977, 1979, 1982 by The New York Times
Company, reprinted by permission), and the *National Review* (© by
National Review, Inc., 150 East 35th Street, New York, NY 10016,
reprinted by permission); "The Baseball Players" in *Atlantic;*
"Couplet" in *The New Republic*, reprinted by permission; "Ping
Pong" in *Inside Sports;* and "Basketball: The Purest Sport of
Bodies" in *Yankee Magazine* (reprinted with permission from Yankee
Magazine, copyright 1984, Yankee Publishing, Inc., Dublin, N.H.).

ISBN: 0-440-32438-6

Reprinted by arrangement with North Point Press
Printed in the United States of America

March 1986

10 9 8 7 6 5 4 3 2 1

WFH

*Dedicated to the memory of my father
and to the company of my son*

Table of Contents

Introduction

Half of my poet-friends think I am insane to waste my time writing about sports and to loiter in the company of professional athletes. The other half would murder to take my place.

My obsession with sports began a year or two before my obsession with poetry, I suppose in mimicry of my father and in companionship. The first essay in this book talks about those days. Like other boys I wanted desperately to be an athlete, but, although (and probably because) I conceived that my father was prodigiously athletic, I was wholly incompetent: I dropped the ball; I struck out; I practiced the airball layup. A few years back, trying to write songs for a composer, I made this lamentation:

> In the baseball game of life
> It's the bottom of the ninth:
> We trail, bases are loaded, and I'm up.
> The pitcher throws a slider
> Just where the plate gets wider.
> I think, I swing, I foul it off my cup.
> Then he brings it *Ex*press Freight
> Through the fat part of the plate.
> I think, I swing, I pop the baseball up.
>
> In the basketball game of life
> I am standing at the line:

> Time's gone. I've got two shots to win the game.
>   In the silent, breathless gym
>   My first one hits the rim.
> I pause, I bounce the ball, I take good aim.
>   If I make it we will tie
>   But my shot hits only sky.
> We lose. I disappear. I change my name.

In a third stanza, I dropped a game-winning pass at the end of the fourth quarter. I ended:

> They can shoot me if they want to. I don't mind.

The last stanza provided the song's low point, both in morale and in poetic achievement. Football is not my favorite sport.

Baseball is, with basketball coming up fast on the inside. And I enjoy both sports on television. Sports for me provide an island at the end of the day, an enclave that is most emphatically not-literature, that is domain of the anti-self, like William Butler Yeats's imagined fisherman who was simple and flicked an expert wrist (Yeats was wristless); it is the place where the child walks. . . .

Everyone needs to find some place in life where the child can walk. . . . No doubt booze is the favorite hobby of the American writer; it is a relaxation area I used to visit. It is highly effective, of course, but bad for the liver in the long run, and in the short run bad for tomorrow. Other avocations cause collapsed veins, lung cancer, and perforated septa. Of course, there are pastimes that do not kill the body: philately, book collecting, adultery, bird watching. . . . T. S. Eliot read a mystery story every night before he slept. Instead of donning Connemara cloth and murdering trout, Yeats read American westerns. Alas, I cannot follow these poets because of my finicky loathing for bad prose. Instead, I entertain the malapropisms of Howard Cosell.

Ten years ago I quit teaching and turned to free-lance writing full time. My perfect day starts at four or four-thirty A.M., with black coffee and the *Boston Globe* (especial attention devoted to Peter Gammons). Then I work on poems as long as I can. I work

best earliest in the day—it's downhill all the way after seven A.M.—
and I care most for poetry, so I give poetry my earliest hours. But
seldom can I work on poetry very long. By eight in the morning,
I turn to something else: maybe a sports piece for a magazine, a
textbook, a juvenile, a book review, an anthology for Oxford, a
short story, an article on anything in the world; first drafts, second drafts, . . . twelfth drafts, . . . proofs, copy editing, . . . letters
about something I am writing or something somebody else is writing, letters gathering information for further work. I work all day,
maybe half an hour each on twenty projects, seldom more than an
hour altogether on one task. Midday after lunch I take a twenty-
minute nap and resume the day. I interrupt writing to read, often
something I will write about, often in a disinterested spirit.

All day I indulge myself in writing and reading. To come down
from this excitement would require a bottle of Scotch. Fortunately,
I cannot drink. My method for achieving calm—allowing the baby
to tire itself out—is to watch Larry Bird on Channel 4, or listen to
radio baseball, or undergo soccer or tennis—or football when there
is nothing else to undergo. Although I like watching the real game
and love Fenway Park and Boston Garden, Boston is two hours
away. So, mostly, I watch the tube. . . . I do not require a daily
anodyne; I do not need particular teams: the game's the thing. I do
not even need whole games.

But I need to leave behind my own ambitions, struggles, and
failures; I need to enter the intense, artificial, pastoral universe of
the game, where conflict never conceals itself, where the issues are
clear and outcome uncertain. I enter an alien place, or the child in
me does—and the child *plays*. . . for a little while. In baseball season, sleepiness overcomes me by the fifth inning. Next morning in
the *Globe*, Peter Gammons will tell me what happened. . . .

So if you use sports to relax from writing all day, why do you
write about sports?

I contradict myself. . . .

We write best where we feel strongest. We write best out of love
and misery, out of hate and bliss. But we also write with pleasure,
and maybe pleasurably, out of feelings less extreme: out of affection

3

or lifelong fascination. We write in order to investigate, to learn, to explore what fascinates us. Free-lance writing is a marvelous way to enter forbidden professional places, to penetrate the secret society as an invited guest. Some years ago I did a profile of Henry Moore for the *New Yorker*, product of the coincidence of two lines in my life: I had loved Moore's sculpture since I first encountered it at the Festival of Britain in 1951; and I had learned how to write prose by doing a book of reminiscences, some of which the *New Yorker* had published, and Mr. Shawn mentioned that he would like me to write more prose for his magazine. When I arrived in England, I was astonished to find that the commission to do a *New Yorker* profile gave me entry at a thousand doors. I already knew Moore, but now I found gallery owners, museum directors, sculptors, painters, and art critics eager to talk with me. The late Lord Clark, merely Sir Kenneth in those days, invited me to lunch at his Saltwater Castle in Kent, where Thomas à Becket used to crash on his way to the Continent. It is fair to assume that the drawbridge would not have been let down for me had I not worn the *New Yorker*'s colors.

I should also add a sporting note to fit this occasion. The Clarks lived mostly in one corner of the ruined castle (thirty rooms or so). In another intact corner, Sir Kenneth kept his study next to a large library; although stacks stuck out from the walls, the middle of the room afforded space for exercise. Atop several huge orientals, Sir Kenneth and Lady Clark had set up a badminton court.

For decades I knew that if I wrote about sports, I could walk into its locked room. But I felt shy. Once I made a tentative and incompetent move toward writing about professional football (see "The Goalposts of Life," the last essay in this book); once I tried to convince Bump Elliott, who coached Michigan football, to let me *inside* for a season—practice, locker room, game travel—in order to report on the game from an intimate viewpoint. He thought the proposition over and decided that my presence would be disruptive.

It took my friend and literary agent Gerard McCauley to get me

4

into the locker room—I tell about spring practice with the Pittsburgh Pirates in "Fathers Playing Catch with Sons." My friendship with Dock Ellis, a product of that week, led me to spend parts of two seasons with the Pirates and to write the book excerpted here in "The Country of Baseball." As a result of these publications, magazines hired me to review baseball books. Here I have revised these book reviews into a piece about sports writing, about prose style, and about storytelling, mostly in baseball—a game that has appealed to many writers. Thus, in "Proseball," I allow myself to peach some good anecdotes.

A couple of these reviews were directed to an English audience (I have retained here a few references to cricket). When John Gross, then editor of the London *Times Literary Supplement*, asked me to become that institution's baseball correspondent, I accepted the honor without hesitation. I expected to print business cards with raised letters, possibly in gold leaf:

> *Donald Hall, Esq.*
> *Baseball Correspondent*
> *Times Literary Supplement*
> *London, United Kingdom*

I planned to flash the card in press boxes from coast to coast. But before I placed my order, Mr. Gross departed for another line of work, and his successor as editor of the TLS, when he saw my second baseball bulletin, became suddenly aware—"Oh Dear," his letter began—that he lacked the space to print it.

Occasionally I did pieces for other magazines, including the late *Inside Sports*. One day my editor there telephoned and asked if I would do a piece on Wayne Gretsky. I was be-deadlined; I did not want to fly to Alberta; and, although I had grown up on hockey, ignoring basketball, in recent decades my affections had reversed themselves. For these good reasons I declined the assignment. After I hung up I worked on a textbook for a few minutes, but my heart wasn't in it; I called the editor back. Picking another remarkable rookie of that year (no one was so spectacular as Gretsky) who played his game down the road in Boston, I asked: How about

Kevin McHale? Thus I was privileged to sit courtside for the 1981 play-off series between Boston and Philadelphia (after which, in an anticlimax, Boston beat Houston for the championship).

What a pleasure that was. And what pleasure, for one who has seldom done it, to hang around the locker room talking with athletes and around the press room talking with reporters. Once I spent a happy day at spring training with Roger Kahn, although we slightly frustrated each other: I wanted him to talk about baseball all day and he wanted to talk about poetry.

D. H.
Wilmot
New Hampshire
23 May 1984

BASEBALL

Fathers Playing Catch with Sons

═══════════◯═══════════

1

1 March 1973

But I don't *want* to go. Work feels good. I am writing poems again. I don't *want* to leave Michigan in March, go to Florida, and run around bases all day in a baseball uniform making an ass of myself.

Three months ago, Gerry McCauley asked me to spend a week of spring training with the Pittsburgh Pirates. I accepted, knowing that things like this never happen. Gerry daydreams a lot.

I make reservations. I cancel appointments. I do back exercises.

But, all the same, baseball . . .

It began with listening to the Brooklyn Dodgers, about 1939 when I was ten years old. The gentle and vivacious voice of Red Barber floated from the Studebaker radio during our Sunday afternoon drives along the shore of Long Island Sound. My mother and my father and I, wedded together in the close front seat, heard the sounds of baseball—and I was tied to those sounds for the rest of my life.

We drove from Connecticut to Ebbets Field, to the Polo Grounds, to Yankee Stadium. When I was at college I went to

9

Fenway Park and to Braves Field. Then, in 1957, I left the East and moved to Michigan. At first, I was cautious about committing myself to the Tigers. The Brooklyn Dodgers had gone to Los Angeles, of all things, and whom could you trust? Al Kaline? Rocky Colavito? Jim Bunning? Norm Cash? I went to Tiger Stadium three or four times a year, and I watched Big Ten college baseball frequently, especially in 1961 when a sophomore football player named Bill Freehan caught for Michigan and, as I remembered, hit .500. The Tigers signed him that summer.

All summer the radio kept going. I wrote letters while I listened to baseball. I might not have known what the score was, but the sound comforted me, a background of distant voices. If rain interrupted the game, I didn't want to hear music; it was baseball radio voices that I wanted to hear.

Baseball is a game of years and of decades. Al Kaline's children grew up. Rocky Colavito was traded, left baseball, became a mushroom farmer, and came back to baseball as a coach. Jim Bunning turned into a great National League pitcher and retired. Norm Cash had a better year at thirty-five than he had had in nearly a decade. And Kaline kept on hitting line drives.

And Jane and I met, and married, and in 1972 the sound of baseball grew louder; Jane loves baseball too. The soft southern sounds of announcers—always from the South, from Red Barber on—filled up the house like plants in the windows, new chairs, and pictures. At night after supper and on weekend afternoons, we heard the long season unwind itself, inning by inning, as vague and precise as ever: the patter of the announcer and, behind him, always, like an artist's calligraphy populating a background more important than the foreground, the baseball sounds of vendors hawking hot dogs, Coke, and programs; the sudden rush of noise from the crowd when a score was posted; the flat slap of a bat and again the swelling crowd yells; the Dixieland between innings; even the beer jingles.

We listened on the dark screen porch, an island in the leaves and bushes, in the faint distant light from the street, while the baseball cricket droned against the real crickets of the yard. We listened while reading newspapers or washing up after dinner. We listened in bed when the Tigers were on the West Coast, just hearing the first innings, then sleeping into the game to wake with the dead gauze sound of the abandoned air straining and crackling beside the bed. Or we went to bed and turned out the lights late in the game, and started to doze as the final pitches gathered in the dark, and when the game ended with a final out and the organ played again, a hand reached out in the dark, over a sleeping shape, to turn off the sound.

And we drove the forty miles to Tiger Stadium, parked on a dingy street in late twilight, and walked to the old green and gray, iron and concrete fort. Tiger Stadium is one of the few old ballparks left, part of the present structure erected in 1912 and the most recent portion in 1938. It is like an old grocer who wears a straw hat and a blue necktie and is frail but don't you ever mention it. It's the old world, Tiger Stadium, as baseball is. It's Hygrade Ball-Park Franks, the smell of fat and mustard, popcorn and spilled beer.

As we approach at night, the sky lights up like a cool dawn. We enter the awkward, homemade-looking, cubist structure, wind through the heavy weaving of its nest, and swing up a dark corridor to the splendid green summer of the field. Balls arch softly from the fungoes, and the fly-shaggers arch them back toward home plate. Batting practice. Infield practice. Pepper. The pitchers loosening up between the dugout and the bullpen. We always get there early. We settle in, breathe quietly the air of baseball, and let the night begin the old rituals again: managers exchange lineups, Tigers take the field, we stand for "our National Anthem," and the batter approaches the plate. . . .

My son Andrew is eighteen years old. Today he telephones from college, and I tell him what I am about to get into. He snickers. I am always doing things that he half wants to deny and half wants to boast about.

He recalls for me the time at Tiger Stadium when, in front of everybody, I dropped a home run that miraculously hurtled into

11

my hand. We were sitting in right-field upper-deck boxes, and a Kansas City left-hander swung hard, and the ball sailed toward me as fat and spinless as a knuckleball. I felt as if I were setting Explorer down on the moon—four, three, two, one—and then it hit. For some reason, I tried to catch the ball one-handed, and it bounced off my left hand with a fleshy crash, a noise like a belly-flop from the high tower, and careened out, over the rail, to the grandstand below. Some 54,000 fans mixed ironic cheers with ironic boos. "Sign him up," I heard around me, and my palm blushed and puffed up.

"Have a good time," says Andrew on the telephone. "You're crazy."

Then my daughter Philippa, who is thirteen, comes to the house for supper. I tell her where I am going. She asks if I can send her a crate of oranges. She is irritated that I am going away from a Michigan March to the sun of Florida, to swimming. Suddenly at supper she looks panicked. "But Daddy," she says, "suppose you *make* the team?"

She has played the flute for a year and a half. "I have as much chance of making the team as you have of playing the flute with the Boston Symphony right now."

"Oh," she says. Then she laughs, but I can see that I have hurt her feelings. She has daydreams too.

2 March

We fly to Atlanta, then to Athens, Georgia, where I will read my poems at the University of Georgia. I have a friend there, a poet named Coleman Barks. He is a fine poet and a good athlete, as poets go. We meet from time to time on the road to read our poems, and he beats me at ping pong. He plays tennis in tournaments.

Now Coleman asks me questions. "What will you do if they ask you to arm-wrestle?"

"It all began in the eighth grade," I tell him. "When I tried out for the baseball team, they didn't *cut* me, they just *laughed* at me." (I remember the faces: "Go home, Hall.")

"That's why I started to write poems," I say. "The humiliation. I could not be good at anything in sports, so I looked around to see what else I could do, to get attention. Especially from girls. Especially, a year later, when I was at Hamden High, from cheerleaders."

"That's not why I started to write poems," says Coleman. "Who do you think you are, George Plimpton?"

I have known George Plimpton for a long time. I edited poetry for his magazine, the *Paris Review*. I decide to call him from Coleman's and ask for advice.

Freddy, who is George's wife, answers the phone. George is out of town. In point of fact, George is in Scottsdale, Arizona, where he is making a movie about shock absorbers. He is making a movie about shock absorbers to be shown to shock absorber salesmen.

The poetry reading seems to go well, though my mind is on other matters.

3 March
Morning. Today we will fly from Georgia to Florida.

Coleman's son Benjamin is nine and reads biographies of Lou Gehrig and Babe Ruth. At breakfast I tell him eagerly about my forthcoming tryout. Benjamin looks uncomfortable.

Daydreaming on the airplane, I realize that I am lacking in quiet dignity. Lou Gehrig had it. Gary Cooper had it. *William Bendix* had it. I must get it. Another time, it might be useful to work up some quiet flamboyance, or even a touch of noisy dignity—but not when you're just starting.

We arrive at the Sarasota-Bradenton airport. I confide in the cabdriver. He tells me that his buddy drove Dick Allen from the same airport to the White Sox training complex. Reading a newspaper later, his buddy learned that Dick Allen signed a three-year contract for an estimated salary of $750,000. Allen gave my driver's buddy a fifty-cent tip.

At the motel on the edge of the Gulf of Mexico, halfway between Sarasota and Bradenton, I give the driver two dollars.

Now I am lying in the sun beside the Gulf, tired but unhappy. I have just hit a tennis ball with Jane for fifteen minutes. I am exhausted. Tomorrow I will put on a uniform at Pirate City in Bradenton. I am terrified. The jokes go away and the eighth-grade faces come leering back. My palms sweat.

Other people start arriving. Gerry is full of plans, does not seem nervous, and I feel worse. I try to frighten him; I frighten myself. I go into a corner and mope. John Parrish the doctor will arrive tomorrow, and Jim Wooten, who writes a column for the *Philadelphia Inquirer*. I don't belong here. I hate everybody. I don't want to have a drink. Everybody else drinks. They are all *regular*. I am weird. I call George Plimpton.

George answers the phone. I tell him, rapidly and apparently in accents of panic, what I am up to. George seems concerned for my spirits. "Why are you whispering?" he says. "You seem to be telling a secret."

But he agrees to give me advice. He suggests that I *listen*—a lot.

"You mean that I shouldn't talk?" I say.

"Yeah," says George. There is a pause. "Do they know who you are, Donald?" he says.

I say I don't think so.

He says the best thing is to cultivate somebody in particular on the team, take him into my confidence, and rely on him for advice, comfort, and support.

"I wonder if I know anyone on the Pirates," he says. "Do I know anybody?"

I let him think about it.

"No," he says.

There is another long pause. He can't think of anything more to tell me. Or perhaps it is difficult for him to phrase his final piece of advice. "Oh," he says, ". . . above all, Donald . . . don't be *solemn*."

"Oh," I say, "yeah. I guess I sound sort of *solemn*, do I?"

"You sound," says George, "as if you were entering the Valley of the Shadow of Death."

2

4 March

Practice on Sunday begins at noon, leaving time for church.

We arrive at Pirate City a little late. In the parking lot, we walk past a dense cluster of Mustangs and sportier objects. Then we see Supercar, a huge Cadillac with a Lincoln grille, cream and red, only the red is a rich and pebbly leather. Leather on the *out*side? No, it has to be vinyl. This is a car that doesn't take any shit. On the license plate we read the owner's name: DOCK.

We find the public relations man, Bill Guilfoile, who will look after us. He takes us to the clubhouse. Nervously, he separates Jane from the rest of us, asking a little old man to take her to the stands. Women are not allowed even *near* the clubhouse.

It's a damp morning, even at noon. The sun starts to burn through. I feel helpless and foolish as I see the little groups of players, young and lean, walking lazily, gathering together in the outfield. I wish I were somewhere else. Or possibly some*one* else. The valley of the shadow of death locates itself in my stomach.

Bill Guilfoile introduces us to the trainer, Tony Bartirome, to the man who runs the clubhouse, and to the equipment manager, who seems incredulous of measurements. I think a forty-two might be best. He shakes his head. A forty? The head keeps shaking; I start to shake. A thirty-eight? He can find a thirty-eight.

Yet once again, I lament obesity. I weigh 226 pounds. Within the past year, I have weighed 238 pounds and 204 pounds. Why can't I keep away from Taco Bell, Arby's, McDonald's, Burger King, Scottie's, Jack in the Box, Red Barn, and H. Salt? Why can't I stay at a nice, comfortable 187? I feel so melancholy about my bad eating habits that I am suddenly overwhelmed with hunger. I look around in panic. There is not a soggy bag of french fries in sight.

My reverie is interrupted by a suggestion from the equipment manager. It will take him a moment to find a uniform; why don't I go out among the players and look around? So I do. Gerry stays behind in the clubhouse, finding reason to talk longer with club officials.

Out the clubhouse door, I see the players gathered in center field.

I walk toward them over the damp healthy outfield grass, aware of my tourist costume: striped Bermudas from J. C. Penney, leather sandals with a peace sign over the instep, and a short-sleeved shirt. Everyone else out here is wearing a baseball uniform.

I stay on the outskirts of the group in center field. There are maybe fifty players in the group, which shapes itself like an amphitheater, with Bill Virdon the manager talking softly to them, outlining the day's activities. A few players look at me, mildly curious—normally, the fences keep out people who look like me—and then look away.

Just as Virdon comes to a close, a large black player with 17 on his back walks over to me, slaps me gently on the stomach, and says with a mock concern, "*Say*, you better do some *laps*!" Suddenly everybody is running. Number 17 beckons me to follow. I start off. I run. I start in the middle of the pack but soon drag to the rear. As we pull around third base, I see my first fans. They look puzzled to see a civilian doing laps with the players. Jane is grinning and hiding at the same time.

As for me, I am elated. By the time I have done a hundred yards, my body hurts but my spirit flies. I know that when Number 17 challenged me he was teasing; taking him literally was teasing him back. By the time I struggle back to center field at the end of the second lap, I am exhausted, but I feel like a free man. Or I feel that illusion of freedom which a drunk man must feel when he runs onto Yankee Stadium eluding police and tries to shake the centerfielder's hand while forty thousand fans boo and clap.

More of the players turn and look now. Number 17 sees me struggle in (he's half an hour ahead of me) and looks surprised. "You really did it," he says. Calisthenics begin. I stand in the back row, near a player with a vacant expression and lots of hair (later, I find out he is Bob Robertson), and I bounce up and down swinging my arms, bend, stretch, lie down, and do it all again. During a pause in the calisthenics, an older man in front of me (a coach named Mel Wright) turns around and says, "Some fine running out there."

"They didn't lap me!" I say.

"It's been a long time since anybody's been lapped out here," he says. "Thought it was going to happen for a while there."

Calisthenics again. Bob Robertson is working hard. Suddenly I see two civilians with cameras dangling all over them. They gesture at me to move closer to Robertson. I oblige and continue my exercises. They bend into their reflex cameras and snap away. I am a novelty photograph.

The loosening up over, I feel as loose as an unraveled sweater. I struggle back to the clubhouse and put on number 43, the road uniform of a coach (coaches have bigger stomachs) named Don Leppert. I meet Bill Mazeroski, gray and leathery as an old greyhound, tough and funny. I meet Steve Blass, who points midsection at Gerry and me, and shrieks: "Look at those boilers!" Learning quickly that we are a bunch of writers, Steve Blass asks plaintively, "Maybe you guys can tell me, what should I do when I grow up?" Blass is thirty-one, the Pirates' best right-handed pitcher for several years past.

In uniform, I discover that my sense of calm and control increases. I feel as if I could walk into bullets. I am aware that my happiness now is as absurd as my earlier terror.

Outside, the players have split into many groups, practicing different parts of the game. Some players throw lazily together, loosening their arms. Everyone must do this every day; if you don't loosen gradually, you will pull a muscle. Others, already warmed up, start to hit against the mechanical pitcher in a little Quonset hangar next to the clubhouse. Distantly, figures run on the four diamonds of the practice field, raising dust. Since it is closest, I go to the batting cage.

The sun is high and hot. Number 17 is leaning against the net, watching Manny Sanguillen take some cuts. From my hip pocket I pull (as surreptitiously as I am able—thirty-eight pants on a forty-two-inch waist make subtlety difficult) my press book on the Pirates. Number 17 is Dock Ellis, owner of the Cadillac with the Lincoln grille and the red leather trim *out*side. I remember *him*; he is a right-handed fastball pitcher, and in 1971, at the All Star break, he was the hottest pitcher in the National League while Vida Blue was the sensation of the American. He made waves when he said the National League wouldn't start him because they would never start a brother against a brother. Naturally, he was called a radical, though it seemed mere realism; he turned out to be imperfectly prophetic, however; he did start against Vida; maybe it was an example of self-defeating prophecy. Later, he made more waves when he complained that the Pirates wouldn't hire him a bedroom with a long enough bed.

I was pleased that it was Number 17 who had slapped my belly.

Manny Sanguillen's face is extraordinarily mobile, his eyes and mouth swimming like fish. When he sets himself for the pitch, he becomes tense as a sprinter at the starting block, listening for the gun that will snap him loose. Extraordinary held-back power—total tension releasing total power—and then absolute relaxation. When Sanguillen drops the bat, takes off the batting helmet, and strolls out of the cage, his whole face lapses slap-happily into humor; he joshes with his friends, a little Spanish and a little English mixed.

"You want to take a turn?" Someone is talking to me. It is a blond young man in uniform, a nonroster player.

"Sure," I say. The sudden jolt in my chest starts as fear and ends as excitement. Sanguillen beckons me and I step inside. The structure is long and low, with a curved roof and an open end (with a wire net) where I had been watching. At the other end, a machine pitches out of the shade, while one of the coaches feeds baseballs into it.

There are several sorts of pitching machines. The old-fashioned kind, still in use, looks as if Rube Goldberg designed it. A mechanical arm, stiff as a cricket-bowler's, finds a ball in its palm, whirls it overhand, and hurls it at you. These old machines are not so fast nor so tricky as the machine here. Another alternative is the miniature howitzer, which uses compressed air to fire baseballs about six miles directly up into the air ("a major league pop-up"), giving infielders and outfielders practice in judging high fly balls. (It also looks as if, fired into low-hanging clouds, it might make rain, or even hail the size of baseballs—maybe even hail with stitches on it.) This howitzer, leveled and pointed somewhere near the batter, becomes a pitching machine; but it is not quite so good as other pitching machines: it is less accurate, not always so fast, and lacks fiendish spin.

The pitching machine that I face is expert in the matter of fiendish spin. Its lethal moving parts are two automobile tires. Well, they *look* like automobile tires, for a small automobile—especially for the sort of small lopsided automobile that characters drive in the funny papers: little doughnut-tires, only these are symmetrical. Probably, in private life, they are automobile tires. As a pitching machine, they recline horizontally, nearly touching each other, spinning in opposite directions at about 120 miles per hour, so that an object dropped between them, at the back, is squashed between them and ejected forward at a terrifying speed. The ball is compressed and expelled from these rotating wheels like a murderous pea from a mad scientist's mechanical pea-shooter.

I stick a hard hat onto my head, the protective flap over my left ear. It is difficult to find one big enough to fit over a full head of hair. I pick up a couple of bats until I find a light one. I know that I will have difficulty meeting the ball, and a light bat will at least be quicker to move. Give me a Willie Stargell bat, thirty-eight ounces, and I will have difficulty lifting it off my shoulder and will gradually sink and topple under its weight.

Outside, I hear ballplayers exhorting other ballplayers: "Come here!" "Watch this!" I spread my legs wide apart, far back in the box, in order to have more time to pick up the ball. I stick my head forward, over the plate. "Stand back!" shout three or four voices in unison. Gene Alley, I am quickly told, had his hand broken two years ago by this same machine.

I thought they took them out and shot them if they did something like that.

I take a practice swing. It's as if I dropped my pants in an old burlesque house—screams of laughter, hoots, catcalls, more shouts to distant ballplayers to come and get a load of this.

But I am too concentrated on the task at hand to allow myself to feel humiliated. The coach loads the machine with baseballs, loading the killer, the mad-dog machine.

I touch the first ball; I graze it as it hurtles past, wrist high, inside, and supersonic. A cheer breaks out behind me. I miss the next one—more cheers. The next one comes in waist high and outside, and I swing early but a little high. I bat it into the ground. Still, I get enough of it so that my right hand feels broken into several parts.

Now that I have the secret, I dig in. I relax. The pitching machine, as if I have made it angry by hitting a ball so that it goes forward, rears back and blows a fastball at my head. That thing dusts me! The *bean* ball! It sticks one in my *ear*!

While I am picking myself up from the muck of the floor, I hear waves and torrents of laughter rising around me. Now the whole team has assembled to see me bat. It seems as if someone had quickly dispatched a bus to Sarasota and assembled the White Sox also. I have become an immensely comic figure; the mantles of Charlie Chaplin and Groucho Marx, possibly of Chico and Harpo also, have descended upon my plump shoulders. Every motion I summon is intrinsically risible. I cannot move a finger, I cannot blink an eye, without plunging a hundred athletes into hysterics. Possibly Tony the trainer will have to subdue them with tranquilizer darts.

When I stand up, I feel more determined than ever. I dig in, and I stare. I concentrate. The ball flings out. When it is perhaps halfway, a voice close to my ear and a little behind me shouts, "Swing!" I do what I am told. I hit the ball solidly, and it goes on a line back at the machine, goes back to the hole it came out of, and strikes the machine. I am even! The ballplayers sing out a cheer. I set myself again, and the voice tells me, "Swing," and I swing, and I connect again.

The first lesson. In a moment, when the coach is picking up baseballs to refill the machine, I look around. The voice at my ear is Dock Ellis, grinning like a jack-o'-lantern. "You're doing real good," he says, "going to make the team." Then he moseys off. So do most of the rest of them, but I take another twenty cuts or so, missing a few, fouling and tipping a few, hitting a few cleanly, trying always to start my swing early and guide it toward the ball as I am swinging. (Keep your eye on it.) Finally my hand hurts so much that I stop.

Later in the day, my hand looks like an inflated red rubber glove.

The day drifts on. I borrow a glove from a ballplayer who looks sixteen. He is practicing running bases. Then, when he wants to field, I give him back his glove, but he offers his backup glove. He tells me I can use it all the time. Very kind of him. His locker doesn't have a name over it, but it is right next to N. McRae, and his glove has "L. Wrenn" lettered on it.

There are no doors or locks on the lockers. Everything is there for the stealing, but stealing is not a problem. The lockers of the older and more famous players—W. Stargell, S. Blass—are full of shoes and mail, tons and tons of mail to answer. I feel an impulse to steal one of Willie Stargell's shoes. Imagine it bronzed and hanging from the mirror over the dashboard of the car! I resist the impulse.

Four diamonds surround a central gazebo, with fenced alleys down the sides of each diamond; the alleys hold fans and a few benches. Each of the four home plates backs up to the gazebo at the center, and the outfields widen away from it like a key lime pie sliced into four pieces, the rim of the pie plate the outfield fences. On one of the diamonds, Don Leppert is bellowing balls into the air from the howitzer. I ask him if he has notified the Civil Aeronautics Authority. "Yeah," he says. "Sure. Yeah."

There is a little pitcher's section between two of the diamonds, a series of rubbers sixty feet six inches away from a series of home plates. Pitching coach Mel Wright watches three young men warm up to pitch batting practice. I recognize the pitcher Nellie Briles, surprisingly short, with a tough and meaty face. On another diamond, a minor league manager hits fungoes to an outfielder, while infielders practice cutoffs, and a rookie runs bases. One diamond is empty.

On another diamond—the one where the old pros usually hang out—Bill Virdon is working on signs and on base running. The player takes a lead at first base. At a sign from Virdon, he lights out for second. Maz Mazeroski is coaching at third. Sometimes he raises his arms to stop the player as he rounds second; other times he waves him into third and puts his arms low for a slide; other times he waves him around third. The player never knows. There is laughter and lightness as Maz crosses up some of the players, waving them frantically around second and third, then stopping them, his arms raised suddenly and flapping like a manic policeman, just as they round the bag. Huge men tear around third and slam the brakes on two hundred and twenty pounds of violent flesh. They look like animated cartoons, spasmodic and exaggerated.

However light and comic the feeling, these men work fiercely. Vic Davalillo, I read in the press book, is going on thirty-four years old; he is slim and quick, but he concentrates on his body like a jeweler with a glass clutched into his eye. When Willie Stargell—huge and strong and slow, with bad knees—runs around second base, one feels the passion of the aging body, digging, pushing, extending itself into pain for the sake of its dignity. Of all the players at Pirate City, Stargell is most impressive. He speaks little, and then he speaks with care and chooses words slowly and exactly. There is a sadness to him, something *blue*, and a strength of spirit that feels even stronger than his strong body. At the same time, along with his strength of spirit, and maybe accounting for it, is the inevitable defeat.

A young ballplayer runs around the bases like a great water-walker skimming over the water, seemingly without effort. Old players shake their heads with admiration and nostalgia, to see him charge, stop, and charge with swift and easy skill. But I watch the old ones, the athletes without the talented young bodies. I watch the intense and concentrated pushing of the self past the self's limits. It is like writing poems, or it is what writing poems ought to be if you are going to last as a poet; you have to bring everything to the poem that you have ever learned, as to the painting if you are a painter or to the swing of the bat if you are a hitter, and everything that you could ever do. You have to push up to the limit, and then past the limit.

Dave Ricketts pauses beside me. I say something of what I am thinking. He nods. "That's what Roberto did," he says. Everyone's

22

uniform has a black bow on the left sleeve in mourning for Roberto Clemente, who died in January of this year.

I wander over to an empty diamond. I walk on the hard red dirt around home plate. Somebody has wetted it down this morning. I walk along the white stripe to first base and touch the bag with my right foot as if I were tagging it on my way to second. It is so large! I wonder why people don't break their ankles tagging it. Then I take a lead, and I stretch my legs as we did earlier in calisthenics, or the way a pinch runner does. Suddenly, without knowing I am going to do it, I light out for second base. It's like the beginning of the four-forty when I was sixteen and running at school. Approaching second, I lean to my left to help myself turn, but run past the bag anyway, and, starting toward third, find myself veering further out, toward where the shortstop would be if there were a shortstop, and when I hit the outfield grass I am exhausted. I cannot catch my breath, I feel panicked for a moment, I want to fall down but I know it is best to keep walking.

I turn around and stroll back toward the center. An old man and an old woman are watching me curiously. When they see that I look back at them, they turn away.

Tomorrow I will be in better shape. Tomorrow when we do the laps before calisthenics, I will get out there and *push*.

I pick up a fungo bat, find Gerry, and start hitting flies. Mostly hitting them; sometimes I miss them. Hitting seems amazingly easy. I throw the ball up with my left hand, grab the fungo bat with both hands, connect, and the ball leaps off the bat. Why wasn't it like this when I was fourteen? Sometimes the connection is like the feeling when you hit a good serve in tennis, the sense of hitting that comes down your arm through your shoulder and into your whole body. Suddenly I am melancholy, thinking of all the missed pleasures—the pleasures of being a young man and an athlete. Why did I omit to be an athlete? For the moment, I forget how hard I tried.

Absorbed in the pleasures of connecting, watching my friends chasing and catching the ball far away on the deep grass, I do not notice that a man with a television camera strapped to his shoulder is aiming his lens at me. He kneels and photographs my fungo hitting. The minute I realize he is there, I miss the ball. He records the empty lunge, smiles, and stands up.

Now it's my turn to field, while Gerry hits. I wear my "L. Wrenn" glove and chase flies. I don't like this part so much. I catch a few and misjudge a whole lot; I cannot throw the ball worth a damn. The TV cameraman follows me into the outfield and records my further adventures in baseball. Gerry tells me it's a Pittsburgh station, Channel 4.

I love it.

Then I watch batting practice for a while, standing in back of the cage to see the balls zoom in and to watch the contracted necks and shoulders uncoil and snap into the ball. Later, I am assured, we will have our own batting practice, with live pitching.

I am exhausted. I sit in the shade, my back against the wire fence. I hear some spectators behind me: "What's that one?" one of them says. I realize that I have crossed some borderline between species; to the spectators, I am an object and I cannot hear—or at least I cannot understand English.

The spectators are old: skinny old men, old women wearing handkerchiefs over their hair. Some of them have their grandchildren with them. Every day they come to practice, watching the athletes throw balls to each other, run bases, and practice with a bat.

While I sit exhausted in the shade, a little boy dares to dart out from a gap in the fence; he points a pencil at me and a pad of paper. It is a moment I have waited for—yet I am embarrassed. "I'm not a ballplayer," I say.

"Huh," he says.

It is too hard to explain. I reach for his pad and write "Don Hall." He runs back through the fence, the successful criminal. Behind me, I hear murmurs. The boy's voice is high pitched, querulous, questioning, disappointed; I cannot hear his words, but I know the burden of the message. His grandfather, however, will not be out-Pirated, not in connection with Pirate History, Pirate Facts and

Figures, or Pirates Past and Present. I hear the confident, elderly, male voice, heavily knowledgeable and reassuring:

"Sure, I know him. He used to catch for the Pirates, years ago."

After I have rested, and stiffened, I think we must be almost ready for our batting and infield practice. But I can hardly move. I find Gerry and play catch with him. Players are drifting back in the direction of the clubhouse. Fans begin to gather around and watch us, looking puzzled. When we pause, I walk over to the fence to call through to Jane, waving as I approach her. An old man in a straw hat sitting next to her waves back, thinking I am waving to him. He looks pleased.

The pitchers are running more laps. Mel Wright, who will pitch batting practice for us, supervises the running. Dock Ellis walks up to me and says with apparent indignation, "What are you doing standing around? You come down here and *run*." So I run. Bruce Kison yells out, "Want to see a grown man vomit?" I don't think I like Bruce Kison.

You run about fifty yards down field, run around a pylon, which is actually Maz Mazeroski disguised as a pylon, and run back. As I approach Maz, I realize that, slow as I am, I don't know how to turn. I may keep running until I hit Tampa. "How do you turn?" I yell at Mazeroski.

"That's all right," says Maz, possibly not understanding my question, "but hit it hard going back."

I lie down then.

Mel Wright comes back, carrying a leather bag full of baseballs. He laughs when he sees me lying down. "Meditating," he says. "Are you meditating to get in shape?"

I struggle to my feet.

"How are you doing?" he says. "Pretty stiff?"

"Not yet," say I. "Tomorrow."

He shakes his head. "Yes," he says, "but the worst time is about the third day, I think." Mel is my age. A player who looks about thirty walks by. Mel calls out to him, "What do you think is the worst day? The third?"

"The fourth," says the other player. Kison walks past. "Look at him," says the thirty-year-old, pointing at Kison. "Couple of years ago he was running around here like nothing bothered him. He's drag-assing it today. I was damned glad to see him drag-assing it today."

Fielding is total humiliation.

I don't care.

The remaining spectators hang on the wire and hoot. Mel Wright hits grounders to the bases in turn. I hang around second. When he hits me a grounder that stays low, it scoots under my glove. I cannot bend that far. Others come bouncing along like rabbits with hideous intent. Invariably, they bounce off the hard dirt to an unpredictable elevation—and careen into my shin or smash into my forearm. The times my back does not allow me to bend far enough and the ball swoops under my mitt, those are the only times without pain. Otherwise, I simply collect bruises, hard little purple knots on my various limbs. My body already hurts so much I do not even care. I embrace my wounds. I am Saint Sebastian.

Then it is time for batting practice. Mel Wright, old pitcher, moons the ball up slowly. I dig, concentrate, swing, feel the sudden ache of my right hand as I connect. (All day the coaches have been examining the puffy red palm and commiserating; the players all wear golf gloves, at least at the start of training.) And when I connect and follow through—my long flat swing modeled in my dreams on Ted Williams with his swing as precise and swift as an electric can opener—usually the ball trickles back toward the pitcher's mound. I am expert at the deceptive art of the swinging bunt.

A few line drives reach the outfield grass, and fly balls make it to second base. I love the feel of hitting the ball when you strike it at the moment when your weight shifts into it and then follow through. Still, my old wrists are not quick enough, even for Mel's moons; I cannot pull the ball. I keep trying, battling with the pain of my right palm. It is painful to grip the bat, as later it will be impossible to grip a doorknob.

Then, just as I am about to retire, for a day at least—Jock for a Day, that's what I am—I suddenly see a reason for keeping at it. Bill Virdon, manager and old center-fielder, begins to walk across our diamond, crossing the foul line behind first base, walking on the soft outfield grass just past the dirt of the infield. When Mel throws his next pitch, I dig in really hard (Virdon is looking this way) and take a mighty cut, and remove my eye from the ball, and miss it, and twist my legs and fall down. I stand up quickly and get into the stance again, barely hearing the laughter. Mel pitches. This time I connect, my best wood of the day. A line drive curves out in the direction of Bill Virdon, who is nearing second base. His clipboard still under his arm, he leaps high in the air to try to catch the ball in one bare hand, his body suddenly lithe as a dancer's, twisted a little, and seeming to pause like a dancer's in midair. But the line drive is a little high and a little to the right. It goes over his head, drops into right field, and dies.

I do believe it would have been a hit. After all those moons, I finally get a single.

3

When I drag-ass back to the Sea Horse, I go to bed. It is four-thirty. I sleep. At six-thirty I try to get up: none of my limbs work; I cannot bend any part of my body; my right hand looks like a peeled muskmelon.

I roll onto the floor and begin to move my legs very slowly. After half an hour, I am able to walk. I can go out to eat, providing I use my left hand for opening doors, greeting strangers, and lifting menus or glasses. Walking is difficult. A bone spur in my left heel is acting up, and I have to walk tiptoe. Walking tiptoe does strange things to shin muscles. I realize that tomorrow is going to be ghastly. But this discomfort is only *there*, like the Gulf of Mexico; it is a place where I am living, for the moment. No big deal. The big deal is that I feel so happy.

At dinner, the visiting imposters begin to know each other. Jim Wooten talks about playing baseball in high school. John Parrish has arrived and watches us all with an alertness which has no threat to it. Suddenly, sitting at the table trying to cut my beef with my left hand, I hear John Parrish ask me, "Did your father play baseball?" I never learn why he asks me, but it lets things loose in me that I have had dammed up for years.

My father and I played catch as I grew up. Like so much else between fathers and sons, playing catch was tender and tense at the same time. He wanted to play with me. He wanted me to be good. He seemed to *demand* that I be good. I threw the ball into his catcher's mitt. Atta boy. Put her right there. I threw straight. Then I tried to put something on it; it flew twenty feet over his head. Or it banged into the sidewalk in front of him, breaking stitches and ricocheting off a pebble into the gutter of Greenway Street. Or it went wide to his right and lost itself in Mrs. Davis's bushes. Or it went wide to his left and rolled across the street while drivers swerved their cars.

I was wild. I was *wild*. I had to be wild for my father. What else could I be? Would you have wanted me to have *control*?

But I was, myself, the control on him. He had wanted to teach school, to coach and teach history at Cushing Academy in Ashburnham, Massachusetts, and he had done it for two years before he was married. The salary was minuscule and in the twenties people didn't get married until they had the money to live on. Since he wanted to marry my mother, he made the only decision he could make: he quit Cushing and went into the family business, and he hated business, and he wept when he fired people, and he wept when he was criticized, and his head shook at night, and he coughed from all the cigarettes, and he couldn't sleep, and he almost died when an ulcer hemorrhaged when he was forty-two, and ten years later, at fifty-two, he died of lung cancer.

But the scene I remember—at night in the restaurant, after a happy, foolish day in the uniform of a Pittsburgh Pirate—happened when he was twenty-five and I was almost one year old. So I do not "remember" it at all. It simply rolls itself before my eyes with the intensity of a lost memory suddenly found again, more intense than the moment itself ever is.

It is 1929, July, a hot Saturday afternoon. At the ballpark near East Rock, in New Haven, Connecticut, just over the Hamden line, my father is playing semipro baseball. I don't know the names of the teams. My mother has brought me in a basket, and she sits under a tree, in the shade, and lets me crawl when I wake up.

My father is very young, very skinny. When he takes off his cap—the uniform is gray, the bill of the cap blue—his fine hair is parted in the middle. His face is very smooth. Though he is twenty-five, he could pass for twenty. He plays shortstop, and he is paid twenty-five dollars a game. I don't know where the money comes from. Do they pass the hat? They would never raise so much money. Do they charge admission? They must charge admission, or I am wrong that it was semipro and that he was paid. Or the whole thing is wrong, a memory I concocted. But of course the reality of 1929—and my mother and the basket and the shade and the heat —does not matter, not to the memory of the living nor to the bones of the dead nor even to the fragmentary images of broken light from that day which wander light-years away in unrecoverable space. What matters is the clear and fine knowledge of this day as it happens now, permanently and repeatedly, on a deep layer of the personal Troy.

There, where this Saturday afternoon of July in 1929 rehearses itself, my slim father performs brilliantly at shortstop. He dives for a low line drive and catches it backhand, somersaults, and stands up holding the ball. Sprinting into left field with his back to the plate, he catches a fly ball that almost drops for a Texas leaguer. He knocks down a ground ball, deep in the hole and nearly to third base, picks it up, and throws the man out at first with a peg as flat as the tape a runner breaks. When he comes up to bat, he feels lucky. The opposing pitcher is a side-armer. He always hits side-armers. So he hits two doubles and a triple, drives in two runs and scores two runs, and his team wins 4 to 3. After the game a man approaches him, while he stands, sweating and tired, with my mother and me in the shade of the elm tree at the rising side of the field.

The man is a baseball scout. He offers my father a contract to play baseball with the Baltimore Orioles, at that time a double-A minor league team. My father is grateful and gratified; he is proud to be offered the job, but he must refuse. After all, he has just started working at the dairy for his father. It wouldn't be possible to leave the job that had been such a decision to take. And besides, he adds, there is the baby.

My father didn't tell me he turned it down because of me. All he told me, or that I think he told me: he was playing semipro at twenty-five dollars a game; he had a good day in the field, catching a ball over his shoulder running away from the plate; he had a good day hitting, too, because he could always hit a side-armer. But he turned down the Baltimore Oriole offer. He couldn't leave the dairy then, and besides, he knew that he had just been lucky that day. He wasn't really that good.

But maybe he didn't even tell me that. My mother remembers nothing of this. Or rather she remembers that he played on the team for the dairy, against other businesses, and that she took me to the games when I was a baby. But she remembers nothing of semipro, of the afternoon with the side-armer, of the offered contract. Did I make it up? Did my father exaggerate? Men tell stories to their sons, loving and being loved.

I don't care.

Baseball is fathers and sons. Football is brothers beating each other up in the backyard, violent and superficial. Baseball is the generations, looping backward forever with a million apparitions of sticks and balls, cricket and rounders, and the games the Iroquois played in Connecticut before the English came. Baseball is fathers and sons playing catch, lazy and murderous, wild and controlled, the profound archaic song of birth, growth, age, and death. This diamond encloses what we are.

This afternoon—March 4, 1973—when I played ball and was not frightened, I walked with the ghost of my father, dead seventeen years. The ballplayers would not kill me, nor I them. This is the motion, and the line that connects me now to the rest of the world, the motion past fear and separation.

4

5 March

The next morning, it takes me an hour of little movements before I chance the big movement of lifting my knee up. Out at the park at ten—up since seven—I am able to run the two laps. Barely. I start out, as I plan, at the head of the pack, and by the time I get to home plate, at the middle of the first of the two laps, I am last.

And every day, in fact, I get slower. My legs feel heavier and heavier. Both ankles turn weak, as if I had turned them recently, though I haven't. Neck and shoulder muscles, from swinging the bat, get creakier and creakier. Only my right hand hurts less, and my heel. Tony the trainer pats an inch and a half of foam rubber in the heel of my left shoe, so that the bone spur gives me less trouble. Otherwise, everything simply gets worse. And people continually ask me how I feel. Pirate City is a convention of hypochondriacs. Everyone monitors his muscles, the shape he is in. Coaches and players alike express astonishment at my deplorable condition. That second morning, Dave Ricketts, who had apparently managed to avoid noticing it the day before, blanches in the clubhouse: "Boy, are *you* out of shape!"

The younger players seem proud of their easy condition, as if youth were virtue. The young players tease the older ones who puff, especially all the old relief pitchers with little potbellies—Ramon Hernandez (thirty-three), Dave Giusti (thirty-four). Still, the old ones are on the roster. Most of the young ones will spend the summer in Charleston, West Virginia, or Sherbrooke, Canada. Only one in five will become a big leaguer. And when that fortunate one in five has made it, he will begin to puff, and he will hear the hungry generations behind him, hurrying to tread him down.

Once I went to an old-timer's game, a few innings of the great players of decades past played before the regular game. The Cincinnati team from 1953—some fifteen members of it—played against a potpourri of retired players from other teams.

The generation of ballplayers slightly older than me, the ballplayers of my childhood and youth, magically returned in their old uniforms and joked and flipped the ball and swung at the slow pitches that the old pitchers lazed up to them. Mickey Vernon played first base, who had played major league ball in the thirties, the forties, the fifties, and the sixties. Carl Erskine pitched. Johnny Mize swung the bat again. Tommy Henrich at fifty-nine stood slim and erect in left field as he had stood for thousands of afternoons in Yankee Stadium. A ball sailed over Gus Bell's head in center field. He plodded after it, his gait heavy and ponderous and painful, while an old catcher dragged himself all the way to third and stood there puffing and gasping. It was grotesque, all of it, like elephants at the circus that waddle and trudge in ballet costumes while the calliope plays *Swan Lake*.

Yet there was an awkward and frightening beauty to the tableau, as the old men performed stiffly the many motions they had once done nimbly. An old third baseman underhanded the baseball toward the pitcher's mound, as he trotted into the dugout, so that the ball rolled to a stop on the dirt near the rubber; how many thousands of times had he made that gesture in the long summers when he was twenty and thirty?

And Pee Wee Reese played shortstop. I was stunned by Pee Wee because I had known him the longest, from the summer of 1940, when he came up to Brooklyn, until he quit in Los Angeles in 1958. Now he stood at shortstop again, fifty-four years old, leaning all his weight on one slim leg, in a gesture almost effete and certainly graceful.

Suddenly I remembered a scene in grave detail from the beginning of my baseball time. It is a Sunday afternoon, 1940 probably, or possibly 1941, when the Dodgers will win the pennant and meet the Yankees in the series and I will see the first game. My father and my mother and I are riding in the Studebaker, listening to Red Barber broadcast a crucial game between the Dodgers and the Giants. The Giants are ahead. Now the Dodgers begin to come close—maybe they tie the game; I don't remember the details—and the Giants stop, pause, confer. Then they summon Carl Hubbell from the bullpen.

My father explains how momentous it is that Carl Hubbell should pitch relief. Things have not gone well for him lately. But King Carl is the greatest left-hander of all time, who, in the 1934

All Star game, struck out Babe Ruth, Lou Gehrig, Jimmie Foxx, Al Simmons, and Joe Cronin, all in a row; he's an old screwballer who walks always with his left elbow turned into his ribs, his arm permanently twisted by his best pitch. The great man seldom pitched relief, and now he walked from the bullpen to the pitcher's mound and took his tosses; old man who had pitched since 1928, who couldn't have more than three or four dwindling years left in his arm; old man come in to save the game for his faltering team.

My father's face is tense. He loves the Dodgers and not the Giants, but he loves Carl Hubbell even more. My father is thirty-seven years old in 1940. So is Carl Hubbell.

Then the Dodgers send up a pinch hitter. It is Harold Reese, the baby shortstop, former marbles ("pee-wees") champion of Louisville, Kentucky, fresh from the minor leagues, and fifteen years younger than Hubbell. I sit in the front seat cheering the Dodgers on, hoping against hope, though I realize that the rookie shortstop is "good field no hit."

Pee Wee hits a home run off Carl Hubbell and the Dodgers win.

Sitting there in the front seat, eleven years old, I clap and cheer. Then I hear my father's strange voice. I look across my mother to see his knuckles white on the wheel, his face white, and I hear him saying, "The punk! The punk!" With astonishment and horror, I see that my father is crying.

This morning a Sarasota newspaper, reporting on the Pirates, told its readers that a bunch of writers had descended on camp, were in uniform, and were going to write a book about spring training. The one with the beard, the newspaper said, was a poet. (The newspaper mentioned the House of David. All my days in uniform, fans keep pointing at me and mentioning the House of David. I suppose at Three River Stadium probably only a handful of fans would have heard of the House of David; but the fans in Florida are old.) Today the fans at the ballpark yell "hey, poet!" at me.

Arthur Daley is here today. He pays no attention to me.

Pittsburgh television, on the other hand, follows me every place. As I pull up a bad last doing laps, I find the man with the camera strapped on his shoulder leveling his mechanical eye at me. Now when I settle into watching the players practice, Myron Cope catches me. Cope used to be a writer for *Sports Illustrated*, and he now does sports reporting for Pittsburgh television. He is visiting the Pirates to do a series of interviews for the nightly news.

Myron Cope asks me if I have written any poetry yet about the Pirates.

No.

Would I write a verse right now?

Huh?

Well, he wants to interview me so that they can have a close-up, for the loyal fans in Pittsburgh, of the figure they have photographed running, hitting, and fielding; Myron thinks it would be a good idea if I made up a poem to recite during the interview.

Sure.

(Poets are always being asked to do poems on ceremonial occasions. You are supposed to come out with a sudden poem, at the banquet the night before the wedding, the way other people are supposed to make toasts. Long ago, I gave up trying to convince people that it takes me a long time to write a poem and that I have to wait for the poem to come to me. Nobody believes you; everybody thinks you're a snob. Years ago, I learned to make jingles on such occasions.)

I set out to make a limerick for Myron Cope. I walk up and down in my baseball uniform, with my ballpoint pen and my ballpark notebook, trying out rhymes:

An out-of-shape poet named Hall

I decide that false modesty is not the order of the day. True modesty, I can only suppose, would not have leapt at the prospect of being interviewed on television.

*Couldn't hit, run, or throw a base-*BALL

Base-BALL was how my New Hampshire grandfather said it. Come to think of it, it was how Robert Frost said it, too. I played softball

34

with Robert Frost in 1945 when I was sixteen. But that's another story.

> *But, in Bradenton,*
> *Runs around in the sun. . .*

And I couldn't get a last line.

So I go and do the interview anyway, faking a last line that I will pretend I forget. Myron Cope, when I finish the limerick, says he doesn't think it will win any literary prizes. . . .

As the interview begins, Myron Cope says that no, the Pirate farm system has not gone crazy (apparently the interview will follow a montage of my prowess in the field), and then he explains what I am up to. Then he asks me what I think of the team, and I find myself talking about effort, and dignity, and the struggle to make yourself worthy.

The players are calling me Abraham.

Dock Ellis turns around, sees me. "Hey, Abraham," he says, "you really a poet?"

I tell him yes. He shakes his head. It takes all kinds.

"Now I see what you guys are doing," he says, referring to the piece in the paper. "You guys ought to get more *involved*."

"How do you mean?"

"You ought to play a game with us."

I tell him we'd like to, but they won't let us. They're afraid of injury, and, anyway, the managers figure the ballplayers ought to take spring training seriously; we'd just get in the way.

He shakes his head. "I'd like to pitch to you," he says. "It'd just be like BP." I register: batting practice. "Except you wouldn't hit me."

"What do you mean?" I say, "of course I'd hit you."

"Naw," he says, grinning.

"I'm sure I could hit you."

"Well," he waggles his head, "OK. But if *you* hit *me*, . . ." he pauses a little, "then *I* hit *you*!"

Most of the players are calling me Abraham. Richie Hebner calls me Jumbo.

He's working out in an infield while I'm hitting fungoes in an outfield. A ball gets through the infield and rolls toward me. "Hey, Jumbo," yells Hebner.

OK.

Sometimes, though rarely, players in uniform cross through the fans' alleys on their way to a different diamond. We cause great excitement. Autographs. An old man asks if he can have his picture taken with me, his wife smiling nearby with her Pocket Instamatic. I start to explain that I am not a ballplayer. "I know," he says. "Look. I want a picture, see, with the man who wrote the book."

Jane keeps notes of fans' comments. One day I wear Bob Johnson's road uniform. Two very old men, puzzled at my appearance, consult their programs. "Bob Johnson," says one of them, "two-hundred and twenty-five pounds, six foot two." (These statistics are rather close to my own. However, Johnson is not yet thirty and has arranged his body in a fashion more appropriate to an athlete.) The two old men are silent for a moment. Finally, one says, "It's funny how that hair on the face can be so deceptive."

We develop personal fans. Jane hears an old woman exclaim, "Oh, I just *love* that one with the beard!" When I return exhausted from batting practice, a man and his wife stop me. "You going to be out again tomorrow?" Yes. "Good!"

I talk some more with "L. Wrenn," whose glove I wear. He is eighteen and from a little town in Indiana. He'll be nineteen in April. Luke is his name. He lives all year in a room at Pirate City, answering the switchboard part of the time for his keep. He graduated from high school last June, was drafted by the Pirates, goes to a community college here—and plays ball. Last fall, he played in the instructional league.

Eighteen! My son is eighteen.

Batting practice . . .

About a hundred vultures wheel overhead, coming closer and closer. I am exhausted again at the end of the day. How can they tell?

Today Don Leppert pitches to us. Mel Wright stays around to watch; he shags flies, his long ropy body stretching itself easily over the infield and the shallow outfield, small potbelly carried gracefully. His body leans over, running like a retired racehorse reminiscing, lodges itself under a Little League pop-up, and catches it in the webbed basket of his bare hands.

I miss a couple. Steve Blass is standing behind the cage. "You got no idea," he says, "how much you're helping Leppert's ego." When I have finished hitting I go out to third base to pick up the grounders headed my way, as Gerry, John, and Jim take batting practice. Steve passes me on his way to the clubhouse. "You better hold back on that hitting," he says. "Six guys just quit, they're so discouraged seeing you hit."

Every day, when I go inside at two or three in the afternoon—practice starts at ten in the morning on weekdays, no lunch, but the real ballplayers finish a little earlier—I collapse into orange juice, into a hard-boiled egg, into plastic boxes of chocolate milk. Nothing has ever tasted so good as that first hit of chocolate milk, a rush so beautiful I would rob a filling station for it. On the long table by the entrance there is soup, crackers, and the debris of many lunches. Ballplayers lounge around in stages of undress, eating and smoking and chatting.

I take long showers, trying to simmer the soreness out. I dress slowly, crossing my legs with care and tenderness. I interrupt my task—from one sock to the other, for instance—to get another shot of orange juice. It is a long and delicate, not to say painful, process. Once, when I am dressed and about to leave, Mel Wright comes up, still in uniform, and shakes his head. "If you rush out of the clubhouse," he says, "you rush out of the game." It sounds, the way he says it, like a clubhouse saw.

37

6 March

For a week I train, work out, and hang around. Each day is more painful than the last. And each day I am more happy.

One day I am late. I miss laps. Dock Ellis spies me sneaking into the clubhouse. He is already *back* there, to see Tony the trainer, after calisthenics are over and done with. He looks at me and speaks in excellent high dudgeon: "You think you can come in here any time you want to? You think you can come out here half an hour late? Five laps! And a fifty-dollar fine!"

All day he keeps adding more laps.

When I get dressed and creep like a guilty thing onto the field, the others accost me. Jim McKee, a tall young pitcher with spectacles, is astonished to see me. "Abraham! I thought you got your release!"

One morning, as I do laps, I am not passed by the last two stragglers until midway through the second lap. It is not because I run faster—I get slower every day—but because they were late in getting started. They come up, one on each side of me, and lift me by the elbows. "You look like you need help," says Milt May. They carry me a few steps. When I finally lumber back to center field, I am offered oxygen.

7 March

In the first exhibition game at McKechnie Field in Bradenton, in the first game of the home season in the grapefruit league, the Pirates play the Detroit Tigers. Al Kaline! Bill Freehan!

I am allowed to suit up for the game and to sit in the dugout with the Pirates. I tell Luke Wrenn. He says, "You're going to sit in the dugout?" He shakes his head. "You're going to hear some language you've never heard before," he says, "I'll tell you. Last fall I was really surprised. I'd never heard anything like that before. Of course I suppose a lot of them had been playing all summer and they were pretty tired."

Listening to Luke, even watching his face, is like being in touch with my grandfather's America. One could think of Norman Rockwell—except that there is nothing coy and no kitsch about Luke. *He* is not nostalgic. He is Luke Wrenn, from Concordia, Indiana: if we asked Central Casting for a "type" to play an eighteen-year-old rookie from a small town in Indiana, they would never find anyone who looked and acted the part this well. Luke is funny and gentle and honest and naive, and he is determined to be a major leaguer. He has read every biography of every baseball player in the Concordia library. He knows what they did. He is an outfielder, and he knows that the Pirates have good outfielders. If he can just *hit* . . . "If you have a good stick," he says, "they can't keep you down."

His face is not like the face of a city boy or of a suburban boy. His face makes a sound like a train whistle heard in the middle of the night. It is a steam train.

When I get to the park, I warm up with the ballplayers, throwing back and forth with Luke and with another rookie.

Also, I walk up and down a good bit, in front of the sellout crowd of thousands of fans, jammed in everywhere. I walk down to the bullpen, back to the Pirate dugout, over to the Tigers. Somebody from the stands yells out, "When you going to get a shave?" They don't like the Pirates; it's a rude Michigan crowd, the parking lot full of cars with Michigan plates.

I pass Billy Martin, who is talking animatedly to someone. Without thinking, I wave and smile at him and say "hi." (I've seen him so much, on TV and at Tiger Stadium, that I am under the delusion that I know him.) He smiles back broadly and waves, apparently under a similar delusion. But the delusion cracks, horribly, in mid-smile, as he realizes that he is waving at a fat Pirate with a beard and long hair. I hurry past to get that one over with. Afterwards, I describe the incident to John Parrish. He advises me to use the line: "That phoney, Billy Martin! He's always pretending he knows me!"

It is permitted to fraternize with members of the opposing team before the game starts. I decide to fraternize with Bill Freehan, who is standing there doing nothing.

"Hi," I say, and rapidly introduce myself before he can get away. I have an angle: Freehan attended the University of Michigan.

When he was a sophomore, which was in 1960–1961, I watched him play football in the autumn, and then in the spring I took my young son to the Michigan baseball games. He was extraordinary that year, and he signed with the Tigers for a big bonus at the end of the college season. I tell him that, as I recall, he hit .500 in the Big Ten.

No, he says, .585. In fact, .500 was the old record. It was Moose Skowron who set it.

Oh.

For five minutes or so we chat. He is agreeable. Looking for something to say—and having been questioned all week about my physical condition—I complain about how horrible I feel when I try to get up in the morning.

"How old are you?" he says.

"Forty-four," I tell him. He nods. He does not make a joke. Freehan is thirty-two. He is lean, tan, and strong. He looks fine. His bat is lively. But I am sure that he feels old. He hears the cleats of the twenty-year-olds behind him. No matter what you do, no matter how hard you work to keep in shape, your body ages. The athlete at thirty-two begins to live in a pain that the athlete at twenty knows nothing about.

And what will he do when he grows up? Every day, I remember Steve Blass's remark. Of course, there is a lot they can *do*, but that is not the point. Growing up means ending what their lives have always aimed for.

Walking around, I find Bill Slayback, a young Tiger pitcher who came up from the minors in midseason in 1972 and who pitched several remarkable games. I congratulate him. With a modesty only slightly weary, he tells me that, after all, it's a long season. I recall that his star dimmed, a bit, in the late going. He is not worried about what to do when he grows up. He is worried that he will not make the team. He is worried that he will grow up too soon.

I sit in the dugout, next to Luke, and wait for the game to start. I suspect I seek out Luke because he is the only person here as naive as I am.

We are at the far end of the dugout. At the end nearest home plate is the water fountain. The water fountain! I remember Red Barber in 1940: "Leo goes over to the water fountain, gets himself a drink. . . ." Above the water fountain, the day's lineup is Scotch-taped to the wall. Also against the wall there is a fierce NO SMOKING sign, by order of the National League. Still, all during the game, the players smoke. They lean back into the dugout when they smoke, so that fans (or Bowie Kuhn or somebody) won't see them. They pass the cigarette around like a joint.

Just before the game begins, the umpires climb into the dugout. Explosive greetings among ballplayers and umpires: "What you been doing all winter?"

"Oh, refereed a couple hockey games. Drank a lot of beer. You?"

"Yeah. Nothing much."

"And I moved. Left Toledo, Ohio, and moved to Syracuse, New York."

"You shouldn't of. Toledo is a good pussy town."

I find myself surprised; I thought that the players were fierce sons, the umpires gloomy and forbidding fathers. But they're exactly the same.

After the "Star-Spangled Banner" and a tribute to the memory of Roberto Clemente, suddenly the dugout is all flurry and bustle. Everyone rummages among bats, pads, and gloves. People at work. The first game of the year.

Squatting for a while near the fountain, I put my glove down. Then I pick it up and move to the end of the dugout to get out of the way. Suddenly a young man with a mustache approaches me. I recognize Richie Zisk, an outfielder. He snatches the glove from where I have it tucked under my arm and turns away. I am flab-bergasted. What does he want Luke's glove for? Then I realize I must have picked up the wrong glove by mistake. I follow him, babbling and embarrassed. "Is that your glove?" I say.

"That's right," he says.

"I must have picked it up by mistake," I say. He says nothing. "I put mine down on the ground," I say. "I must have picked up yours by mistake."

"Anybody can make a mistake," he says tersely.

"I'm sorry," I say. "I'm really sorry."

He says it again as if I hadn't heard him. "Anybody can make a mistake."

He sounds anxious. It is uncertain that he will make the team.

The game. Richie Hebner hits a home run. Everybody in the dugout shakes his hand, though I feel foolish when he looks up and sees it is me. "Jumbo," he says.

Bob Johnson gets hit. Bill Slayback is wild. Manny Sanguillen misjudges everything in right field. The Tigers win it. It's poor baseball, and nobody seems to care. As for me, I am perched in the center of a universe of bliss.

By the middle innings, rookies are playing most of the positions. But not Luke. He keeps walking up and down in front of Bill Virdon, but the magic words go unspoken. Meantime, a Detroit Tiger eighteen-year-old has driven in a run, somewhat aided by Manny Sanguillen's fielding. Another outfielder throws to the wrong base. And in the dugout, no one offers criticism. In fact, the only chatter seems to come from Tony the trainer: "Strike his ass out!" When a rookie center-fielder for the Pirates lets a fly ball by Rich Reese drop behind him for a double, Maz spits three times in rapid succession. That is about as emotional as we get.

I wander down to the bullpen where Bob Miller is warming up. "When I get in there," he says, "I want you to clear away all those photographers. Otherwise it'll be manslaughter."

One of the Pirate scouts, leaning against the bullpen wall in civvies, calls me Babe.

It is a lazy afternoon. Standing out by the bullpen, I hear players talk slowly to each other, spitting, wondering what to do tomorrow. Back at the edge of the dugout, Bob Robertson is chewing and spitting magnificently. When the dugout is full, the arcs of spit are miraculous to behold. Look the length of the dugout at any given moment, and several brown wads of liquid tobacco will be rainbowing out. The cement floor and the cement steps are slimy with spit.

On the other hand, there are the voices, like rain, especially the soft Spanish voices congregating in the center of the dugout—Ramon Hernandez, Vic Davalillo, Manny Sanguillen. The sound of Spanish softly droning, like a distant motor. Like a romantic mosquito.

From the shade of the manager's corner the field looks tranquil, the long lateral green stretching out forever in the afternoon, 342 to left field, 433 to center, 373 to right. But Bill Virdon stands with his foot up, and stares, and does not relent. He is terse. "Bob?" he says. "Left field." And Robertson picks up his glove and jogs out.

I decide to drink the water from this fountain of my youth. I lean toward the water and experimentally twist the knob. A mighty jet stream vaults out, water that could have made the Olympics, and splashes all over Bill Virdon's right leg. He looks over his shoulder at me calmly and silently—and here I am apologizing again, awkward as a virgin—and then he turns back to the field.

I get the idea he thinks I am goofy.

All afternoon, off and on, I talk to Luke, sitting next to him in the dugout. He wants to know about my writing. Maybe I can help him, someday.

How?

Well, just in case . . . he is keeping a diary of his experiences, and perhaps if he is lucky, some day . . . Then he talks about how, last October, he watched the Pirates and the Tigers in the play-offs, and here he is.

He is another son. When you are a teacher, you get used to having extra sons. Baseball is fathers and sons playing catch, the long arc of the years between. Yet I also have my own son, who does not resemble Luke. My own son belongs to 1973, not 1923; reads Castaneda, not biographies of baseball players; frets over no one's dirty language, hitchhikes everywhere, and accepts everything except policemen.

Therefore Luke, if he is 1923, actually resembles my father more than he resembles my son. The moment I think of it, I realize that all along I have thought that he looked like photographs of my father.

The day after the Tiger game, the Pirates play Minnesota at one-thirty. I am exhausted after my morning workout—it is almost the end of my brief career; I am prepared to hang it up; I am a broken man—and I decide not to come to the park for the game. It would be such a letdown to sit in the stands after I had been in the dugout the day before. Late in the afternoon, however, I wander down to the ballpark anyway. Who can stay away?

The Pirates are down 2—o going into the seventh. They score five runs to lead 5—2 and take the lead into the ninth, when Minnesota scores four more runs to go ahead 6—5. When a left-fielder makes a good throw to third base, holding a runner to second after a single, I notice that it is Luke. Really, I am surprised. I didn't expect him to play, not even in the ninth inning of the second exhibition game of the spring. After all, even *he* keeps his ambitions modest and reasonable. He *expects* to play this summer in Bradenton, in the Gulf Coast League, the team lowest on the Pirate ladder; he *hopes* to be noticed enough to be sent a bit higher up, class A, maybe to Salem, Virginia, in the Carolina League. He is in uniform now only because he lives at Pirate City all year long. The players practicing in Pirate City now will soon move to McKechnie Field, and Luke will stay behind at Pirate City with two hundred other minor leaguers.

So I'm surprised and pleased to see him in a game.

He comes to the plate in the last of the ninth, one out and a man on second. He hits the ball cleanly, a line drive just out of the reach of the second baseman. The ball goes into the alley in right center and scores the tying run, and Luke stands on second base with a double after his first time at bat in a Pirate uniform. The next batter hits a ball on which Minnesota manages to commit two errors, and Luke comes home with the winning run.

In less than a minute, Luke is surrounded by photographers and reporters and by kids getting autographs. He keeps grinning. Eighteen years old.

5

9 March

Next morning is my last. Heavy with fatigue and melancholy, I arrive at the clubhouse to find the rain starting. The team bus idles outside the entrance. In theory, the Pirates are driving to Lakeland where they will play the Tigers again. Dock is going to pitch. He tells me that he always likes pitching against the Tigers. Good games, he says, grinning; lots of throwing at hitters.

But not today. It's raining in Lakeland, too, and the bus is waiting for word of a cancellation. The bus will never go. I look inside the bus: smoke and card games. Some of the players, like Dock, wander around outside in the rain. A few run in the mud. Others start to take batting practice with the insane machine in the Quonset. There is an air of restless improvisation, like summer camp when the rains come; what will we *do*?

I go inside to find Luke. He is dressing by his locker, and when he sees me—and he knows what I am going to say—his face loosens into a smile as broad as a barn. No ambiguities. The *Sarasota Herald-Tribune*, this morning, has taken full measure of his obscurity for journalistic purposes, and headlines the game:

BUCS CALL ON WRENN
FOR A 7−6 TRIUMPH

He accepts congratulations without pain and can still talk about where the ball went.

The photographer Bob Adelman, unfamiliar as yet with the arduous path to the majors, asks Luke if this means that he will make the team. For someone of Luke's encyclopedic knowledge of baseball, this is a stupid question. (Luke knows how long it took Ted Williams, where he played in the minors, and what his batting average was for the month of July 1936 in class B ball.) But he answers the question politely. No, he says, it doesn't mean he'll make the team. Maybe it means he'll get to play in class A, where he wants to play. Of course, he says, with his head vanishing under a sudden cloud of daydreams, if they took him on a road trip and he hit twelve for twelve. . . .

I decide not to try to work out in the rain. I change from my uniform back into Bermuda shorts and sandals forever. I look for people to say goodbye to. Standing among the lockers, I feel a pinch on my calf. I look back. Ramon Hernandez looks innocently into space.

Oh, my teammates! How can I leave them!

Here is Dock, who shakes hands and says with great formality and gentleness that it has been real good to know me and that I should look him up at the ballpark. I start to walk to the car, slogging through the instant mud. Then Luke runs up. One more thing! If he does make it, sometime, would we please write him for tickets? He sure would be pleased to see us again.

And I him, and my father and my son, and my mother's father when the married men played the single men in Wilmot, New Hampshire, and my father's father's father who hit a ball with a stick while he was camped outside Vicksburg in June of 1863, and maybe my son's son's son for baseball is continuous, like nothing else among American things, an endless game of repeated summers, joining the long generations of all the fathers and all the sons.

Baseball
and the Meaning of Life

Professor McCormick's suggestion is surely far-fetched. Although black-suited umpires may remind him of warlocks, although the pitcher's motion mimics dubious rituals, we must resist the suggestion that baseball retains elements of the Old Religion. We may admit the existence of "Seasonal Parallels" without lending credence to his speculations on the shape of home plate.

For baseball dies into the October ground as leaves fall, obscuring base path and pitcher's mound, littering empty dugouts and bullpens, flitting like spooked grounders over second base into the stiffening outfield grass. November rain expunges lime-powder foul lines from Centerville's Little League Park to Yankee Stadium, from Yakima to Bangor, from Key West to Iron Mountain. Soon in the north a colder powder, no less white, freezes diamond and foul territory together into an egalitarian alabaster plain below the cold green ranks of box, grandstand, and bleacher. The old game waits under the white; deeper than frozen grass, down at the frost line it waits . . .

. . . To return when the birds return. It starts to wake in the south where it had never quite stopped, where winter is a doze of hibernation interrupted by sleepy staggering momentary wakenings, like bears or skunks in a northern thaw. The game wakes gradually, gathering vigor to itself as the days lengthen late in February and grow warmer; old muscles grow liraber, young arms throw strong and wild, legs pivot and leap, bodies hurtle into bright bases SAFE. . . . Clogged vein systems, in veteran oaks and left-fielders both, unstop themselves, putting forth leaves and line drives in Florida's March. Migrating north with the swallows, baseball and the grass's first green enter Cleveland, Kansas City, Boston. . . .

Silly he may be, but on the whole we sympathize with Professor McCormick's imaginative anthropology (*The Bat and the Wand*, Cooperstown: A. Doubleday, no date). At least we share the intuition that connects baseball with the meaning of life.

2

April baseball is tentative, exploratory, daring and timid together, poking a quivering finger into the risen year. May strengthens, sure-footed now, turning night into bright green day, springing with young manhood's energy and vanity toward the twilights of high summer. In June the animal-plant, full-leaved and muscled with maturity, invites us to settle secure for a season.

We arrive at the ballpark early. The ballplayers have been here for hours, for batting practice and pepper and shagging outfield flies, as coaches with fungoes bang balls at the shins of shortstops, or raise cans of corn to the shallow outfield, or strike line drives off outfield walls and corners. We arrive and settle with score cards and Crackerjack and peanuts and Schlitz and hot dogs. There is a rasp in our voice, there is glory in our infant heart, there is mustard on our T-shirt.

While most of the players drink coffee in the locker room, smoke cigarettes, and sign baseballs, one or two wander on the grass in front of the dugouts. They want to be alone. Or, on the other hand, they want to sign autographs for kids or flirt with girls wearing jeans as tight as their own double-knits. Of the twenty-five players on the roster, these loners number themselves among the least active, though each of them knows that if he played every day . . . Most are young; a few show gray in the beard they will not shave until after the game—utility men, bullpen catchers, pinch hitters.

Then the tunnel disgorges three young men in bright suits carrying gloves, then two more, then six. "Play catch?" one says to another. They sort themselves by twos, throwing baseballs hard at each other without effort, drawing ruler-straight lines like chalk stripes between them. The soft pock of caught balls sounds in attentive ears.

The bullpen squad consists of a coach, a catcher, two long men, and two or three short men; they amble with fabulous unconcern, chewing as slowly as prize Holsteins, down the foul lines toward their condominium in right field. The ninth inning's fastballing superstar ace-relief man is not among them but is back in the trainer's room lying flat on his back, reading *Swann's Way* or *Looney Tunes*, waiting to trot his urgent trot from dugout to bullpen at the start of the eighth, the game 1 – 1, the one-man cavalry alerted to the threat of ambush at the mountain pass.

Anticipating cavalry, the organist assaults the score of the "Star-Spangled Banner," which we attempt to sing because of the fierce joy that fills us and threatens to choke our throats unless we loosen a joyful noise. Then we chew the song's ending and lean forward to watch the young men assume the field in their vain uniforms, to hear "Play ball," to allow the game's dance to receive our beings into its rhythms for two hours or three and then, in late afternoon, to release us again into the rubble of random streets.

Ah, the game! The game!

But what of the meaning of life . . .

3

Baseball connects American males with each other, not only through bleacher friendships and neighbor loyalties, not only through barroom fights but, most importantly, through generations. When you are small, you may not discuss politics or union dues or profit margins with your father's cigar-smoking friends when your father has gone out for a six-pack, but you may discuss baseball. It is all you have in common because your father's friend does not wish to discuss the assistant principal or Alice Bisbee Morgan. About the season's moment you know as much as he does; both of you may shake your heads over Lefty's wildness or the rookie who was called out last Saturday when he tried to steal home with two out in the ninth inning and his team down by one.

And you learn your first lessons of the rainbow arc all living makes but that baseball exaggerates. For when you are in sixth grade, the rook has fuzz on his face and throws to the wrong base; before you leave junior high school, he is a seasoned regular, his body filled out, his jowl rippled with tobacco; when you graduate from high school, he is a grizzled veteran—even if you are not certain what *grizzled* means. In a few years the green shoot becomes the withered stalk, and you learn the shape of the hill all beings travel down.

So Carl Yastrzemski enters his forty-second year. So Wilver Stargell's bones are stiff. While George Brett climbs the glorious mountain of his prime, all gut and muscle, his brother Ken watches with admiration and irony from the shadows of his quick sundown; Ken started the All Star game for the National League in 1974, his record thirteen and two, the lithe left arm bending sliders to catch the black—unbeatable, impervious, in his high stride hitting home runs from the ninth position. His brother George played AAA that year. That year somebody asked Ken Brett, "Why don't you play outfield when you're not pitching?" He smiled from his pleasant height, "Because they do not have that much money in Pittsburgh."

In 1980 Ken was released by the Dodgers and later signed on with George's Kansas City as a long man in the bullpen. This year or next he will begin to make "The Adjustment," as the players call it, when he leaves forever the game he doubtless began at the age of seven or eight. The light grows pale on the older players but never dwindles entirely away. . . . I remember Edd Roush, batting champion of 1917, ancient and glorious at an old-timer's game in 1975.

Smokey Joe Wood, amazing fastballer of the 1912 Red Sox, signed autographs in Boston at a collector's convention in 1980.

Let it be. Players age, and baseball changes, as veterans slide off by way of jets to Japan instead of buses to Spokane. Baseball changes and we wish it never to change. Yet we know that inside the ball, be it horsehide or cowhide, the universe remains unaltered. Even if the moguls, twenty years from now, manage to move the game indoors and schedule twelve months a year, the seasons will remain implicit, like the lives of the players. Grow-lights do not legislate winter away; if the whole sport emigrates to Japan, baseball will remain a Zen garden.

For, surely, as Dr. McCormick fails to remind us, baseball sets off the meaning of life precisely because it is pure of meaning. As the ripples in the sand (in the Kyoto garden) organize and formalize the dust which is dust, so the diamonds and rituals of baseball create an elegant, trivial, enchanted grid on which our suffering, shapeless, sinful day leans for the momentary grace of order.

O Fenway Park

On a wall near the grandstand gates there's a bronze plaque:

NEW
FENWAY PARK
BUILT 1912
RECONSTRUCTED 1934

It's the oldest, and maybe the best, ballpark in the major leagues.

For most baseball fans, maybe oldest is always best. We love baseball because it seizes and retains the past, like the snowy village inside a glass paperweight. Though baseball goes through continual small changes, we do not acknowledge them. We cherish baseball's 1890s costumes and scarcely notice when the double-knits become as form-fitting as Captain Marvel's work clothes. We accept the designated hitter in the American League and plastic grass in the National, as if these innovations were our heritage. Even conservative Fenway Park has added baseball's newest accessory—the message board—and it seems as if it has been there forever.

As you look at the scene outside, you'd never believe that anything was new at Boston's ballpark. Ancient bars, hamburger joints, and souvenir shops jostle each other across from the pitted brick walls. In the streets, vendors of hot dogs, pennants, balloons, peanuts, and illegal tickets cry their wares to the advancing crowd.

The streets carry a sweet, heavy, carnival air, like an old-fashioned marketplace. You half expect to run into a juggler or a harlequin.

Inside Fenway, late afternoon sun illuminates the grass, making it so bright that I squint to see it. I look around at the old park again, green chairs, iron girders holding the roof up—and young ballplayers taking batting practice. I come to the ballpark early to watch BP, the antique and immemorial rituals of batting and shagging flies while pitchers run in the outfield. Especially I come early to *this* ballpark, tiny and eccentric and warm hearted, because I want to look my fill and to remember.

As I look around, the oldest and smallest ballpark in the major leagues renews itself to my eyes, with its crazy angles jutting into the field. It's like a huge pinball machine designed by a mad sculptor, driving outfielders mad when they try to predict a carom. The box seats everywhere lean into the field, disturbing ballplayers who try to catch foul flies. But the closeness is great for the fans. Even general admission in Fenway Park is nearer the field than the box seats in new ballparks. I sat in the center-field bleachers when Luis Tiant opened the 1975 World Series; as he swiveled toward second base in his rotating windup, Luis and I were eyeball to eyeball.

I remember other games and other years. I went to Fenway first in the early forties, when I was thirteen or fourteen, and watched the young Ted Williams, slim as a trout, arc his flat and certain swing. Returning to Fenway every year, I saw him age. In 1948 I watched the one-game play-off between Boston and Cleveland for the American League pennant, won by Cleveland as Lou Boudreau lifted a fly ball into the left-field screen and a line drive into the right-field bleachers—or was it the bullpen? A year later I came with my grandfather, a New Hampshire farmer who had seen the Red Stockings play once before, late in the last century; he had been hearing about Fenway Park for almost fifty years but had never left his haying long enough to see a game. He decided he liked Fenway Park.

The fifties, the sixties, the seventies . . . All these years, Fenway has gone unchallenged. Back in the forties, there was agitation to remove the short left-field wall and take over Lansdowne Street in order to build more bleachers. The Red Sox listened, but it turned out that three different cadres of politicians had to approve any move they made—city, county, and state; it was unthinkable that three sets of politicians could agree on anything so serious.

In the sixties, agitation came from a football team that rented the stadium from the Red Sox, the Boston Patriots as they were. Understandably, they disliked the seating capacity and the sightlines —the best seats for baseball turned up in one football end zone or the other. In Boston newspapers it was bruited that the two teams would collaborate on a new stadium near South Station, with a movable roof and places to park. But when Boston taxpayers heard the projected cost, the rumors scattered and fled. I suspect this pleased Mr. Yawkey, owner of the Red Sox until his death in 1976, who owned Fenway Park outright—no mortgage—and who would never have taken orders from a commission.

It also pleased nostalgic baseball fans everywhere, who wanted no multimillion-dollar trailer camp to replace this antique jewel, this decadent emerald set in the Boston sea. They showed their appreciation, too. In a park that seats only 33,379 people, the Red Sox have led the American League in attendance seven out of the last ten years.

Ten out of ten years, Boston fans have led the league in enthusiasm and madness. They pull me back to Fenway as much as the ballpark does. They're *baseball* fans, knowledgeable and assertive, if a trifle loony. They know their baseball, not from listening to TV commentators but from sitting through hot afternoons in the Fenway bleachers. They make the old green walls palpitate and pulse as their intensity gathers and builds in the pressure of this small cooker. Their numbers include such celebrated eccentrics as the South Boston midget known only as O. O'Sullivan, who hands silver dollars to the fans around him—a dozen each time—when Carl Yastrzemski hits a home run. And there is Lulu from Honolulu, yesteryear's attraction at the Old Howard, who occupies in her dotage a grandstand seat behind the Red Sox dugout.

The reconstruction of 1934, commemorated on the bronze

plaque, didn't reconstruct a whole lot. As new owner, Mr. Yawkey took down the old wooden bleachers and replaced them with modern ones, which hold up pretty well after these many years.

The breakneck urge toward modernization continues apace.

In the winter of 1975–1976, after the great World Series of 1975, the Red Sox assembled a vast bank of lights above the center-field bleachers, an item known as the message board, which can transmit not only messages but pictures—and not only still pictures but moving ones also. Fenway Park becomes an enormous outdoor television set.

If baseball fans are nostalgic and Bostonians traditional, then innovation at Fenway Park is doubly cursed. When the newspapers reported the forthcoming message board, Boston's fans were outraged. Quickly the Red Sox assured everyone that at least the message board would not lead cheers; it would never, they swore, tell the fans CHARGE.

By early June of 1976, everyone in the park accepted the message board as *immemorial*. It had become at least as immemorial as hot dogs and possibly more immemorial than Crackerjack. Now in Fenway Park, after a dazzling play, the dazzle repeats itself in the black air over center field, a grainy rotogravure, gross and miraculous, allowing us to savor again, as we learned to savor in the privacy of our living rooms, exact repetition of the glorious act.

For myself, I was in love with it before the first pitch. Warming itself up, the message board showed us the groundskeepers preparing the infield at the same time that they were doing it. Thirty thousand people had the choice: they could observe the reality—a man named Al Forrester watering down the dirt of the infield—or they could watch, one one-thousandth of a millisecond later, the enlarged and fuzzy image of reality.

On the field Al Forrester strolls stoutly, doing his immemorial job. Above him on a screen, a huge sepia Al Forrester patrols the same acreage, his hose blooming with large drops of water, until suddenly the player at the message board console pushes a button, and an enormous Al Forrester *stops*, sharp, like *that*—his hose and its water petals fixed at a permanent moment—while below on the real field the small man, returned to his merely human body, arrives at third base.

Above him, for more than 30,000 people, a moment of our lives stands stock still—like all the moments of all of us here, irrecoverable in fact but secure in our memories: Ted Williams playing a ball in the left-field corner; Lou Boudreau lifting a fly toward the green wall; my grandfather leaning forward in 1949, his eyes electric in his tanned farmer's face. Therefore we cherish a message board—the one outside our heads to rhyme with the one inside.

The Poet's Game

Everybody knows "Casey at the Bat," that ritual humiliation of the hero. Before radio killed the practice of public recitation, everybody knew it by heart. "Oh! somewhere in this favored land," our foremothers and forefathers boomed out Ernest L. Thayer's bumpety meter, "the sun is shining bright/ And somewhere men are laughing, and somewhere children shout;/ But there is no joy in Mudville—mighty Casey has Struck Out."

Despite Casey's omnipresence, few fans of baseball or poetry seem to have noticed that baseball has always been the preferred sport of American poets. The earliest baseball poem, with the base called a "post," is the anonymous:

> The Ball once struck off
> Away flies the Boy
> To the destin'd Post
> And then Home with Joy.

Well, the poem is *called* "Base Ball." Actually, we know little about the eighteenth-century game. It is typical of baseball scholarship that *Baseball Diamonds* dates these lines 1784; that Charles Einstein in *The Baseball Reader* ascribes to the poem a patriotic year, albeit with skepticism ("Supposedly printed in 1774"); and that H. L. Mencken attributes it to *A Little Pretty Pocketbook* published in 1744.

Mencken is right but neglects to mention that the book was published in 1744 by John Newbery—in England. At least we can be sure that baseball's poetic association started early, long before Abner Doubleday supposedly invented the game. When Henry Wadsworth Longfellow attended Bowdoin in 1824, he wrote in a letter about playing "ball"; presumably this was "town ball," which was baseball's general ancestor, with resemblances to cricket and to the English ball game of rounders.

Among baseball's early fans was the greatest American poet. In 1846 while he was still a journalist, about a decade before Ralph Waldo Emerson welcomed *Leaves of Grass*, Walt Whitman reported about baseball for the *Brooklyn Daily Eagle*. The modern game was just beginning, and Whitman lived to see baseball become national under standard rules. Soldiers of both sides played in the Civil War (there are legends about gray teams playing blue teams during lulls in the fighting), which spread the game and gave credence to the silly notion that a Civil War general invented it. In the first edition of *Leaves of Grass* in 1855, in "Song of Myself," Whitman found place for the great game in his sampler of pleasures: "Upon the race-course, or enjoying picnics or jigs or a good game of base-ball. . ." Whitman doubtless pronounced it, as people did until the 1920s, with the two syllables evenly stressed.

When he was old and ill in 1889 and the Chicago White Stockings returned to the United States from baseball's first international tour, the poet remarked to a young friend, "Did you see the baseball boys are home from their tour around the world? How I'd like to meet them . . . !" The same friend reports that Whitman's conversation featured baseball metaphors: a great success was "a home stroke," and he liked to catch things "on the fly. . . ."

As the game developed in Whitman's old age—accelerating its change, becoming pervasive and nearly uniform—he heard about an innovation that disturbed him greatly, just as the designated hitter and plastic grass disturb the literary fan today. Whitman heard rumors of the curve ball. He spoke to a friend named Thomas Harned, who dropped by to visit him after seeing a ball game.

Whitman asked him if it were true, these days, that "the fellow who pitches the ball aims to pitch it in such a way the batter cannot hit it?" In the game of Whitman's youth, the pitcher served the ball underhanded, and it was his purpose to make it easy to hit. The notion that pitchers would employ *deception* seemed morally reprehensible, unfair, and undemocratic to Walt Whitman. He lamented the state the grand old sport had sunk to: "I should call it everything that is damnable," said the old man.*

Among modern poets, doubtless the most famous fan is Marianne Moore, who lived in Whitman's borough and who cheered the Brooklyn Dodgers. She noticed and admired details of the game, like Roy Campanella patting Don Newcombe's rump. It is less known that her interest in baseball started early, long before the Campanella/Newcombe era. The American poet (and editor of *Others*, 1915–1919) Alfred Kreymborg tells a baseball story about Marianne Moore in his autobiography, *Troubador*, preserving an anecdote of poetry and baseball from seventy years ago. In the early years of this century, around the time of the Armory Show in 1913, Kreymborg hung out with some young American poets who lived in the environs of New York City, from Greenwich Village to Paterson, New Jersey. These figures included Wallace Stevens, William Carlos Williams, several poets currently unread, and Marianne Moore. All were dazzled by Moore's elegant and erudite speech. Whatever subject arose, as they picnicked and gossiped of a Sunday, Moore always knew more about the subject than anyone else and discoursed on it with routine knowledge and sagacity. When Williams and Kreymborg marveled at the range of her information, Kreymborg rashly offered to bet Williams that he could discover a subject on which Miss Moore remained speechless. Williams took the bet. Kreymborg then invited Moore to attend a baseball game between the Chicago Cubs and the New York Giants at the Polo Grounds, where the Giants played their home games.

*I am indebted to Lowell Edwin Folsom's article about Whitman and baseball in the *Iowa Review*, Spring–Summer 1980.

He had reason to believe that the great Christy Mathewson would pitch for the Giants.

As the two poets journeyed to the ballpark on the El, Miss Moore spoke in paragraph form on the subject of poetry. She continued while they took their seats in the grandstands; she continued while Mathewson warmed up and pitched to the first batter, whose name—Kreymborg records it—was Shorty Slagle. Finally Kreymborg interrupted, calling her attention to the field where the handsome right-hander had slipped a called strike past the batter.

"Excellent," said Miss Moore.

Her approbation caught Kreymborg short. He asked her if she knew who was pitching.

"I've never seen him before," Miss Moore allowed, "but I take it it must be Mr. Mathewson."

Kreymborg realized that he had failed to lead Miss Moore outside the range of her erudition. Astonished, he managed to gasp, "Why?"

"I've read his instructive book on the art of pitching," she said, as the umpire called a second strike, "and it's a pleasure to note how unerringly his execution supports his theories."

Moore's own poems about baseball came late in her work; literary critics have been unkind to "Baseball and Writing," and "Hometown Piece for Messrs. Alston and Reese," with its couplets:

> Ralph Branca has Preacher Roe's number: recall?
> and there's Don Bessent, he can really fire the ball.

Others have perhaps done better. Moore's friend, the doctor-poet William Carlos Williams, wrote a good poem in "At the Ball Game," not necessarily kind to baseball fans. Robert Frost, whose boyhood hero was Cap Anson, alludes to baseball in "Birches" among other poems. As an old man he wrote one of his rare pieces of prose to celebrate baseball for *Sports Illustrated*.

In English departments throughout the nation, professors teach courses in sports literature. Freshmen and sophomores face text-book *Suggestions for Discussion and Writing* like "Explain 'Dream of a Baseball Star' by analyzing the imagery in the dream" or "Thomas Jefferson said that 'games played with a ball stamp no character on the mind,' an opinion generally supported by the findings of psychologists. . . . Do such findings invalidate the view of . . . Robert Frost and Marianne Moore?"

These suggestions come from *The Sporting Spirit: Athletics in Literature and Life*, a text edited by Robert J. Higgs of East Tennessee State University and Neil D. Isaacs of the University of Maryland. This book is high-toned, starting out with Pindar and Euripides; when we leave the Greeks, we arrive at baseball poets like Gregory Corso ("Dream of a Baseball Star"). Then there is *Sports Literature*, edited by John Brady and James Hall, with Paul Goodman's "Don Larsen's Perfect Game" ("His catcher Berra jumped for joy") and Rolfe Humphries' "Polo Grounds" ("Time is of the essence. The crowd and players/ Are the same age always, but the man in the crowd/ Is older every season . . .").

In books like these, Robert Wallace makes an elegant little poem about "The Double Play." Ogden Nash rigs out an alphabet from baseball players' names. Robert Francis does brief, exact lyrics on pitchers and base stealers. And the poets keep at it: Carl Sandburg, John Updike . . . not to forget F. P. Adams with his rhyme on "Tinker-to-Evers-to-Chance"—a trio of infielders immortalized not for their fielding but for the metrical utility of their surnames.

In *Baseball Diamonds*, a huge anthology edited by Kevin Kerrane and Richard Grossinger, there are sixty-five baseball poems, most of them contemporary. There's a bunch by Joel Oppenheimer, who once wrote a book about the Mets, and there's a fifteen-page mini-epic on Ty Cobb by William Pritchard, who edits the *New York Quarterly*. The most prolific baseball bard is Tom Clark, who has also written prose books about Charles O. Finley, Mark Fidrych, and Shufflin' Phil Douglas. He writes a little elegy for "Clemente (1934–72)":

61

won't forget	head back
his nervous	on his neck
habit of	like a
rearing his	proud horse

Baseball Diamonds also includes the three baseball poems of Robert Francis, which most of these books reprint. Here is "The Base Stealer":

> Poised between going on and back, pulled
> Both ways taut like a tightrope-walker,
> Fingertips pointing the opposites,
> Now bouncing tiptoe like a dropped ball
> Or a kid skipping rope, come on, come on,
> Running a scattering of steps sidewise,
> How he teeters, skitters, tingles, teases,
> Taunts them, hovers like an ecstatic bird,
> He's flirting, crowd him, crowd him,
> Delicate, delicate, delicate, delicate—now!

The poems, I suppose, share no theme except for love of the game. But why do poets love the game so much? Poet and critic John Crowe Ransom suggests that baseball has the quality of the pastoral—that genre of verse where shepherds sing to nymphs or lament the passing of other singing shepherds—making a world that is small, exact, formal, whole, pleasing, and separate from ordinary reality: a green island in a sea of change. In the best baseball poems the poets pay attention to small things—the way Clemente held his head or how the base stealer picks his moment. These are acts of attention through the microscope of the pastoral: the tiny, entire scene set off and concentrated.

Or maybe it is simply that all of us need regularly to revisit childhood.

In naming the best baseball poems, we must mention "Casey at the Bat" as at least the sentimental favorite. As for the favorite sentimentality, a leading candidate might be Grantland Rice's elegy for Babe Ruth, which once saturated the country with tears as durable as newsprint. "Game called by darkness . . . ," the sports writer begins. He ends his penultimate stanza, "The Big Guy's left us, lonely in the dark,/ Forever waiting for the flaming spark." Of course he saves his best for the last line—making in the process one of the most forced rhymes of literary history: "The Big Guy's gone—by land or sky or foam/ May the Great Umpire call him 'safe at home.'"

For some of us, as we slide toward the ultimate home plate, there is yet another sentimental favorite. In 1907, C. F. McDonald published "The Volunteer"—indebted, it is true, to "Casey at the Bat"—to provide a model for vigorous middle age. The poem describes a match between Bugville, which can field only nine players, and a visiting team, which is both superior and supercilious. Bugville finds itself losing in the top of the ninth when its catcher breaks his thumb, leaving only eight men on the field unless a volunteer from the stands replaces the injured player. "And then a tall and stocky man cried out, 'I'll take a chance.'" Well, with the new catcher—whose "hair was sprinkled here and there with little streaks of gray"—Bugville retires the bullies, comes to bat, and after two outs stages a rally, topped by a winning home run from the volunteer himself. Here is the last stanza:

"What is your name?" the captain asked, "Tell us your name," cried all,
As down his cheeks enormous tears were seen to run and fall.
For one brief moment he was still, then murmured soft and low:
"I'm mighty Casey who struck out just twenty years ago."

The Necessary Shape
of the Old-Timers' Game

For some of us, events like the Cracker Jack Old Timers Baseball Classic are obligatory, ineluctable, and essential. They complete the great game of baseball, extending the diamond's spectrum into vibrations of the ultimate shade.

Maybe some of us are crazy. We prefer an old-timers' game to game one of an ordinary World Series (though probably not to game six, 1975, Boston Red Sox and Cincinnati Reds). Certainly we prefer it to the ordinary All Star game, that annual convention of the mere masters of the moment, when superb athletes at the peak of their form take a day away from pennant races, do a little extra BP, show off a little, and send us yawning to bed.

For some of us, an event in which Luke Appling takes Warren Spahn deep—in *1982*—takes precedence over mere excellence. We applaud the magic of restitution. Bar wrinkles, bar waistlines, bar gimp, bar gray hair and bald head: by a ludic spell we no longer inhabit the 1980s; we wipe mist from the mirror and it is thirty, it is forty years ago. . . . Better still, our magic mixes eras, and there are impossible juxtapositions—as if we introduced Don Quixote to Huckleberry Finn: In Cincinnati a few years back, I watched Willie Mays raise a can of corn to Dixie Walker.

In 1982, the Boston Red Sox, who rarely undertake such things, constructed themselves an old-timers' game. I live a mere two hours north of Fenway Park, in New Hampshire, and wound up with seats under the scoreboard in the center-field bleachers. At Fenway Park such a position is no disadvantage: at least by contrast with symmetrical football stadia like Pittsburgh and Cincinnati, where box seats extend two hours north of home plate.

Most of the ballplayers, that afternoon, looked fit and fine. Maybe Jackie Jensen was a *little* thicker around the middle, but he moved like the old halfback he was. Earl Wilson had a *little* trouble getting the ball up to the plate, but Jim Lonborg didn't. There was Mel Parnell, there was Frank Malzone, Bobby Doerr, Tommy Harper, Walt Dropo, Rick Ferrell (eldest at seventy-seven), Dick Radatz, Jimmy Piersall, Billy Goodman, Rico Petrocelli . . .

Most of all, there was Ted Williams. It was mostly the return of number 9 that filled Fenway Park that day. Forty years ago I discussed Ted Williams with my New Hampshire farmer grandfather (who remembered Babe Ruth pitching for the Sox) while he and I hayed together, hot afternoons of World War II. Even then, we remembered past greatness—.406 in 1941—and we daydreamed about his triumphant return.

In 1982, old number 9 had aged a bit—stiff, portly, gray—yet he retained in his age that languid arrogant athlete's grace which I recalled: the Splendid Splinter, the Kid, Teddy Baseball, who retired in 1960 and hit a home run for his last at-bat. In 1982, at the old-timer's game, he hit his best in BP, a ball that bounced into the right-field stands. During the three-inning workout, he flied to right off Lonborg in the first, then struck out on a high pitch, 3−2, in the third.

The old fellow knew that we wanted him to lose one into the grandstand; trying to oblige us, he struck out swinging mightily rather than take a walk. It was satisfying to see him swing again, even if he missed. The Williams swing was slower but its shape remained intact: a great flat circle looping around itself, coiling the body up in its follow-through.

An old-timers' game is not only magical restitution but also essential shape.

The game of baseball starts in the first light of dawn, as small children swing bats in schoolyards and vacant lots. (These days I spend happy baseball days umpiring grammar school softball games, boys and girls together, on the playing field outside the Danbury, New Hampshire, Primary School; these contests are contentious, polite, and nobody wins by more than ten runs.) Later comes Little League, later junior high. . . . By late morning, in high school, the true athletes begin to detach themselves in the bright light. For some there is then college, for some rookie league and class A, and for a very few the high noon of the major leagues.

For symmetry and shape we require the crepuscular evening baseball of the old-timers' game, where the children of fifty years ago, and the bright heroic twenty-eight-year-olds of our maturity, gather to celebrate in shadow the rituals of noon.

Only a week after playing with the boys of twilight, at Fenway Park in 1982, the stylish body of Jackie Jensen collapsed in death, a sudden heart attack. That afternoon we had watched him thrive. . . .

And in the first inning, we watched as a batter lifted a fly toward Ted Williams in left field, a loping, curving ball, easy to catch but that would drop in front of him if he did not hasten. Slow to start, he stumbled-ran forward; at the last moment, he extended his right hand down toward his ankle and snapped the ball from the air. It was a catch no one would have noticed forty years before, but now it summoned all of us out of our seats, applauding, and weeping as we applauded.

Of course, on the field, in twilight as at noon, the requisite manner was not weeping but teasing. It was Curt Gowdy who said it: "Good field no hit."

The Country of Baseball*

1. Touring the Nation

Baseball is a country all to itself. It is an old country, like Ruritania, northwest of Bohemia and its seacoast. Steam locomotives puff across trestles and through tunnels. It is a wrong-end-of-the-telescope country, like the landscape people build for model trains, miniature with distance and old age. The citizens wear baggy pinstripes, knickers, and caps. Seasons and teams shift, blur into each other, change radically or appear to change, and restore themselves to old ways again. Citizens retire to farms, in the country of baseball, smoke cigars and reminisce, and all at once they are young players again, lean and intense, running the base paths with filed spikes.

Or they stay in the city, in the capital of the country of baseball. At the mouth of the river, in the city of baseball, young black men wear purple leather maxicoats when they leave the ballpark. Slick dressers of the twenties part their hair in the middle and drive roadsters. In old *barrios* everyone speaks Spanish. Kids playing stickball, and kids running away from cops, change into fierce adults rounding third base in front of fifty thousand people, and change again into old men in their undershirts on front stoops.

Though the grass transforms itself into a plastic rug, though the

---

*First chapter of *Dock Ellis in the Country of Baseball*, New York, 1976.

players speak Arkansas or Japanese, though the radio adds itself to the newspaper, and the television to the radio, though salaries grow from workingmen's wages to lawyers' compensations, the country remains the same; everything changes, and everything stays the same.

The players are white and black, Cuban and Welsh and Mississippi farmers. The country of baseball is polyglot. They wear great mustaches and swing bottle-shaped bats, and some of them dress eccentrically. John McGraw's Giants play two World Series wearing black uniforms. Now the citizens' hair shortens, their loose uniforms turn white, their faces turn white also, and the white world cheers—while on the other side of town, black crowds cheer black ballplayers. Now the hair returns—beards, handlebar mustaches, long locks hanging beside the catcher's mask; now brightly colored knickers cling close to thick legs; now bats are scooped out at the thick end; now black and white play together again.

In the country of baseball the magistrates are austere and plainspoken. Many of its citizens are decent and law-abiding, obedient to their elders and to the rules of the community.

But there have always been others—the mavericks, the eccentrics, the citizens of independent mind. They thrive in the country of baseball. Some of them display with Lucifer the motto, "I will not serve." Some of them are known as flakes, and unless they are especially talented bounce from club to club, to retire from the active life sooner than the others. Left-handed pitchers are reputed to be craziest of all, followed by pitchers in general, and lefthanders in general. Maybe 40 percent of the population in the country of baseball is flaky, at least in the opinion of the other 60 percent.

When Al Hrabosky meditates hate, in his public solitude behind the St. Louis mound, he perpetuates a great tradition.

The country of baseball begins to take shape at the age of six. Earlier, sometimes. Dock Ellis's cousin gave him a baseball to hold when Dock was in his crib. But Little League starts at six and stickball and cowpastureball at about the same age. At seven and eight and nine, the players begin to reside wholly in the country of baseball. For the people who will live there forever, the long summers take on form—time and space shaped by the sharp lozenge of the base paths. Then high school, maybe college, maybe rookie league, class A, double A, triple A—the major leagues. In the brief season of maturity, the citizens of this country live in hotels, watch movies, pick up women who lurk for them in lobbies, sign autographs for kids, and climb onto the team bus for the ride to the ballpark at five in the afternoon.

In their brief season, they sit for a thousand afternoons in front of their lockers, pull on archaic stockings, set their knickers at the height they affect, and josh and tease their teammates. Tony the trainer measures a tender elbow, tapes an ankle. Then the citizens saunter without urgency onto the field, gloves under arms, and pick up a ball.

Richie Hebner sees Richie Zisk. "Hey," he says, "want to play catch?"

Baseball, they tell us, is part of the entertainment industry.

Well, money changes hands; lawyers make big money; television people and their sponsors make big money. Even the citizens make big money for a while. But like actors and magicians and country singers and poets and ballet dancers, when the citizens claim to be in it for the money, they are only trying to be normal Americans. Nothing is further from the country of baseball than the business life. Although salaries grow and contract clauses multiply, the business of baseball like the business of art is dream.

In the cardboard box business, a boss's expectations rise like a plateau gradually elevated, an infinite ramp leading to retirement on the ghost plains of Arizona. And in the country of cardboard boxes, the manners of Rotary proliferate: the false laughter, the bonhomie of contracts, the golf played with boss's boss. Few flakes survive, in the country of cardboard boxes.

But in the country of baseball, men rise to glory in their twenties and their early thirties—a garland briefer than a girl's, or at least briefer than a young woman's—with an abrupt rise, like scaling a cliff, and then the long meadow slopes downward. Citizens of the country of baseball retire and yet they never retire. At first it may seem that they lose everything—the attention of crowds, the bustle of airplanes and hotels, the kids and the girls—but as they wake from their first shock, they discover that they live in the same place, but that they live in continual twilight, paler and fainter than the noon of games.

Dock visits an old friend, Alvin O'Neal McBean, retired to his home in the Virgin Islands. In the major leagues, McBean was *bad*. The language of Rotary does not flourish in locker rooms or dug-outs; the citizens' speech does not resemble the honey-tongued *Reader's Digest*; eccentricity breeds with outrage. "McBean would as soon curse you as look at you," Dock says—even if you were his manager or his general manager; and he could *scream*. He was therefore not long for the major leagues. Now Alvin O'Neal McBean supervises playgrounds, the old ballplayer teaching the kids old tricks, far from reporters, umpires, and Cadillacs. "He's made the Adjustment," says Dock. "He doesn't *like* it, but he's made the Adjustment."

The years on the diamond are fantasy. The citizens *know* they live in fantasy, that the custom cars and the stewardesses and the two-inch-thick steaks belong to the world of glass slippers and golden coaches drawn by unicorns. Their fathers were farmers and one day they will be farmers also. Or their fathers loaded crates on boxcars for a hundred dollars a week and one day they too will load crates on boxcars for a hundred dollars a week. Just now, they are pulling down five thousand.

But for them, the fantasy does not end like waking from a dream or like a transformation on the stroke of midnight. They make the Adjustment, and gradually they understand that even at a hundred dollars a week, or even on top of a tractor, they live in a crepuscular duplicate of their old country.

And most of them, whatever they thought, never do just what their fathers did. When they make the Adjustment, they sell insurance or real estate to their former fans, or they open a bar in the Missouri town they came from. They buy a restaurant next to a bowling alley in their old Oakland neighborhood, and they turn paunchy, and tilt a chair back behind the cash register, remembering—while they compute insurance, while they pull draft beer—the afternoons of August and the cold September nights under the blue lights, the pennant race at the end of the dying season.

The country of baseball never wholly vanishes for anyone once a citizen of that country. On porches in the country of baseball old men are talking. Scouts, coaches, managers; car salesmen, manufacturers' representatives, bartenders. No one would let them exile themselves from that country if they wanted to. For the kids with their skateboards, for the men at the Elks, they remain figures of youth and indolent energy, alert at the plate while the pitcher fidgets at the mound—a young body always glimpsed like a shadow within the heavy shape of the old body.

The old first baseman, making the final out of the inning, in the last year he will play, underhands the ball casually toward the mound, as he has done ten thousand times. The ball bounces over the lip of the grass, climbs the crushed red brick of the mound for a foot or two, and then rolls back until it catches in the green verge. The ball has done this ten thousand times.

Basketball is not a country. It's a show, a circus, a miracle continually demonstrating the Newtonian heresy that muscle is lighter than air, bodies suspended like photographs of bodies, the ball turning at right angles. When the game is over, basketball does not continue; basketball waits poised and immobile in the locked equipment room, like the mechanical toy waiting for a hand to wind it.

Football is not a country. It's a psychodrama, brothers beating up on brothers, murderous, bitter, tender, homosexual, ending with the incest of brotherly love and in the wounds Americans carry all over their bodies. When the game is done, football drag-asses itself to a bar and drinks blended whiskey, maybe seven and seven, brooding, its mouth sour, turned down, its belly flowing over its angry belt.

In the country of baseball days are always the same.

The pitchers hit. Bunting, slapping weakly at fat pitches, hitting line drives that collapse in front of the pitching machine, they tease each other. Ken Brett, with the fireplug body, lifts one over the center-field fence, as the big hitters emerge from the dugout for the honest BP. "Did you see *that*?" he asks Wilver Stargell. "Did you see *that*?" he asks Al Oliver.

The pitcher who won the ball game last night lifts fungoes to a crowd in left field—outfielders, utility infielders, even pitchers who pause to shag flies in the midst of running. When they catch a ball, they throw it back to the infield by stages, lazy arcs linking outfielders to young relief pitchers to coaches. Everyone is light and goofy, hitting fungoes or shagging flies or relaying the ball. Everyone is relaxed and slightly self-conscious, repeating the motions that became rote before they were ten. Some citizens make catches behind their backs, or throw the ball from between their legs. Behind the mound, where a coach begins to throw BP to the regulars, Paul Popovich and Bob Moose pick up loose baseballs rolled toward the mound, and stack them in the basket where the BP pitcher retrieves three at a time. Now they bounce baseballs on the cement-hard turf, dribbling them like basketballs. Moose dribbles, fakes left, darts right, jumps, and over Popovich's jumping body sinks a baseball in a wire basket for a quick two points.

Coaches slap grounders to infielders, two deep at every position. Third, short, second, first, a bunt for the catcher. The ball snarls around the horn. Third, short, second, first, catcher. At the same time, the rubber arm of the BP pitcher stretches toward the plate, where Bob Robertson takes his turn at bat. Two balls at once bounce toward Rennie Stennett at second. A rookie up from Charleston takes his cuts, and a shortstop jabs at a grounder from Bob Skinner, and Manny Sanguillen leaps to capture a bunt, and the ball hums across the infield, and Willie Stargell lofts an immense fly to center field. Behind the cage, Bill Robinson yells at Stargell, "Buggy-whipping, man! Buggy-whipping!"

Stargel looks up while the pitcher loads himself with balls, and sees that Joe Garagiola is watching him. Tonight is Monday night. "Hey, man," he says slowly. "What are the rules of this bubble gum contest?" He whips his bat forward, takes a cut, tops the ball, grimaces. Willie has two fractured ribs from a ball thrown by a forty-one-year-old Philadelphia relief pitcher. Philadelphia is trying to catch Pittsburgh and lead the Eastern Division.

"What rules?" says Garagiola. "I don't have them with me."

Willie whips his bat forward with accelerating force. "How many pieces?" He hits a line drive off the right-field wall.

Garagiola shrugs. "Four or five," he says. "Something like that." He laughs, his laugh a little forced, as if he felt suddenly foolish. "Got to have a little fun in this game."

Nearer to game time, with the pitchers running in the outfield, the screens gone from the infield, five Pirates are playing pepper between the dugout and the first-base line. Dave Giusti holds the bat, and fielding are Ramon Hernandez, John Morlan, and Daryl Patterson. Giusti hits miniature line drives back at the other relief pitchers. Everyone laughs, taunts, teases. Giusti hits one harder than usual at Hernandez. Another. The ambidextrous Puerto Rican —who tried pitching with both arms in the same inning until they stopped him; who pitches from the left side now, and strikes out the left-handed pinch hitter in the ninth inning—Ramon drops his glove, picks up a baseball in each hand, winds up both arms as he faces Giusti head on, and fires two baseballs simultaneously. Giusti swings laughing and misses them both.

In the outfield, big number 17 lopes with long strides, then idles talking to fans near the bullpen for ten minutes, then fields grounders at second base, says something to make Willie Stargell laugh, and walks toward the dugout. Seeing Manny Sanguillen talk with Dave Concepcion and Pedro Borbon, soft Spanish fraternization with the enemy, he throws a baseball medium fast to hit Manny in the flesh of his thigh. Manny jumps, looks around, sees who it is, laughs, and runs with gentle menace toward him. But Dock has turned his back, and leans on his folded arms at the top of the dugout, scanning the crowd for friends and for ladies, his high ass angled up like a dragster, his big handsome head solemnly swiveling over the box seats—bad Dock Ellis, black, famous for his big mouth, suspended in 1975 for a month without pay, the suspension rescinded and pay restored, Dock, famous for his Bad Attitude, maverick citizen in the country of baseball.

At Old-Timers' Day in Cincinnati, Edd Roush is an honorary captain, who hit .325 in the Federal League in 1914, .352 in the National League in 1921, and played eighteen years. Lou Boudreau plays shortstop. His gut is huge, but he breaks quickly to his left and scoops a grounder from the bat of Pee Wee Reese, and throws to Mickey Vernon at first. I saw Lou Boudreau, player-manager for Cleveland, hit two home runs at Fenway Park in the one-game American League pennant play-off in 1948. I discovered Pee Wee Reese eight years earlier, when I was twelve, and the soft voice of Red Barber on WOR chatted about the new shortstop up from the Louisville Colonels. Joe Nuxhall pitches, who pitched in the major leagues when he was fifteen years old, and still pitches batting practice for the Cincinnati Reds. And Carl Erskine pitches, and Harvey Haddix. Harvey Kuenn comes to the plate, and then Dixie Walker—who played right field for the Brooklyn Dodgers, and confessed to Mr. Rickey in the spring of 1947 that he could not play with a black man. Dixie Walker flies out to a citizen who retired last year, still limber as a squirrel, playing center field again—Willie Mays.

In the country of baseball, time is the air we breathe, and the wind swirls us backward and forward, until we seem so reckoned in time and seasons that all time and all seasons become the same. Ted Williams goes fishing, never to return to the ballpark, and falls asleep at night in the Maine summers listening to the Red Sox on radio from Fenway Park; and a ghostly Ted Williams continues to play the left-field wall, and his flat swing meets the ball in 1939, in 1948, in 1960. In the country of baseball the bat swings in its level swoop, the ball arcs upward into the twilight, the center-fielder gathers himself beneath it, and *Dixie Walker flies out to Willie Mays.*

2. Pitching and Poetry

I met Dock Ellis and the Pittsburgh Pirates for the first time in 1973. With my literary agent Gerard McCauley and four other unathletic and sedentary men, I had contracted to put on a uniform and participate in spring training—as Paul Gallico and John Kieran and George Plimpton had done before us.

In the season that followed, Dock was twelve and fourteen, with a 3.05 ERA. He was out with a sore elbow late in the season, or the Pirates might have won their division. The Mets edged past them at the end.

That summer I went to night games at Tiger Stadium, and by day I wrote a number of things, including an account of my week of spring training. That autumn, Dock tape-recorded an introduction to *Playing Around*, the book that collected our humiliations in the sun. He wrote about "one guy that had a gut and a beard," and recorded, among other observations, my triumph over a pitching machine:

> So then the poet—the frustrated ballplayer, I can't recall his name—you could tell this guy wanted to play ball all his life and he just knew he could hit the ball so he got in there and he swung about ten times, and I said, "Oh, the bat is getting heavy, huh?" Because, normally, if you keep swinging the bat it will get heavy. So I said, "Turn the machine down," so then he fouled one off and he was so happy he jumped out of the cage and everyone cracked up.

Actually, it wasn't like that at all.

In March of 1974, during spring vacation from the University of Michigan where I teach, I was invited to read my poems at Rollins College in Winter Park, Florida.

For a poet, the poetry reading is the main source of income connected with writing. Magazines pay little; you may sell a poem for $17.50, or give it away, since many poetry magazines pay nothing. And when you do a book, even if it sells moderately well, you will find yourself with only a few hundred dollars in royalties. But then, as if in obedience to Emerson's notion of compensation, some college will ask you to read your poems for an hour, and maybe spend another hour talking poetry with students—and pay you a thousand dollars. The same college has a library unable to afford $4.95 for one of your books.

Nobody would write poems to make a living anyway. But the poetry reading has brought a touch of comfort to the life of the poet. Especially when the reading occurs at the beginning of March, in Winter Park, at the lotus-eating campus of Rollins College—and baseball camps are busy in every nook and cranny of the peninsula.

I spent ten days in Florida, two of them at Rollins College, and eight at Pirate City.

Ostensibly I went to Pirate City to publicize *Playing Around*. Really, I felt nostalgic about the country of baseball, which I had visited so briefly the year before. I wanted to hang around baseball further, and writing about it seemed the only way. I tried to think of things to write.

Meantime, I enjoyed myself. Each morning I hung around the training diamonds, and Dock came over to gossip between doing laps and other tasks. He suggested that he pitch to me *this* year. I told him I couldn't even swing a bat. In fact, I had barely crawled from the bed in our motel on the Gulf; my back was out, lower back muscle spasms, and I feared that my playing days were over. Dock put on a shrewd look. "I know just where to pitch you," he said. "Low and outside."

He told me how he had dictated his introduction, how he had tape recorders rigged up all over his apartment; with them he practiced being a disc jockey, one of the professions he considered taking up when he finishes playing. He spoke all sorts of things into those tape recorders; maybe sometime he'd be doing a *book*.

For a moment I wondered if I was listening to a hint. Then Dock left to join the other pitchers at practice in catching pop-ups, so we didn't carry the question further. The pitchers gathered on one of the four infields at Pirate City, where the compressed-air howitzer pitching machine—which doubles as a fly-ball or pop-fly machine —occupied home plate. One after another, pitchers lay face down on the grass next to the pitcher's mound. Don Leppert would pull the lanyard—or whatever you call it—and boom the baseball high into the dazzling blue air of the Gulf. When the ball went up, Leppert yelled to the pitcher to stand up and catch it. Since he had been lying face down, he had no idea where in the sky to look. His fellow pitchers yelled confusing instructions at him: "Left! Left!" "Behind you!" "Watch out!" "Right!" "No! No!"

Most of the pitchers never found the ball at all. Two were beaned. The crowd of colleagues—each of them doomed to suffer the same indignity—hooted and howled as pitcher after pitcher zigzagged crazily across the infield, jerking this way and that like a lizard cornered by a cat, and searched out the white speck against the bright sky, only to have it crash to the grass beside him. After each round of laughter, bad advice, and catcalls, the new victim would emerge from the chorus, the old one return to its ranks.

"Dock Ellis," yelled Don Leppert. "Dock!" He came forth, hooted at already, sauntering, elegant, and took his prone position. When the howitzer fired, he leaped to his feet and circled the mound. He obviously heard nothing of the misdirections of the others—this was his tenth spring training—and wholly concentrated on distinguishing the little ball. At the last moment, as it fell to the side of him, he flicked out his left hand and caught the ball. He was the only pitcher that morning to catch the pop fly.

Later in the day, going back to the locker room to shower and go home, he was tired and moved slowly. "You were the only one to catch the pop-up," I told him. "Congratulations."

He shrugged. "It just fell in my glove," he said. "I was just protecting my *face*."

Then he looked more serious, perhaps grieved. "I don't *like* the ordeal of catching the ball like that. It's nothing but *killing time*. In a game, the pitcher will *never* catch a ball like that. In a game? *No way!* Third baseman, catcher, *any* infielder. No way they're going to let us catch that ball. It's not practice, even for rookies.

"It's a psychology thing. 'If one of your *infielders* misses a ball

like that'—this is manager Danny Murtaugh talking—'we're letting you know how difficult it is.' Oh, *difficult*."

Dock's speech is emphatic. Trying to render his speech, I use so
much italic that his conversation looks like Queen Victoria's letters. It is difficult to render anyone's speech in print; Dock's is
impossible. He is emphatic, he mimics, he uses grand gesture and
subtle intonation and eloquent facial expression. He also varies
swiftly from black vocabulary and syntax to academic or legal white,
with stops at all stations on the way. His language is so varied that,
if he were a fictional character, he would be inconsistent and unrealistic. Sometimes, maybe, Dock *is* unrealistic. But Dock is real.

I thought about wanting to hang around baseball. I thought about
the enigma of Dock himself—here was this supposedly bad man,
this hostile screaming crybaby of the sports pages; and yet he
seemed to me funny, sophisticated, and friendly. I decided to do a
little hinting of my own.

"You know that book you might do?" I said the next morning.
"If you ever want anybody to read it for you, you know, to help you
revise it or anything, I'd be happy to do it."

Dock turned it back, with one of his apparent changes of mind.
"Oh, I won't *write* a book," he said. He might *do* a book; he
wouldn't *write* one. "You're a writer, aren't you?"

We had smoked each other out.

We stood together in the Florida sun, watching an intrasquad
game together, and talked without joking for two hours; we talked
about basketball—like so many pitchers, Dock was a great high
school basketball player—and about his daughter, and his wife
from whom he was separated, and his boyhood in California, and
even about writing poetry. Dock made a tentative analogy between
the writer using words to influence the reader, and the pitcher's
devices to outsmart the batter. I said I'd think that one over.

Then Dock said good-bye and strolled down the foul line toward
the bullpen, where he warmed up to pitch his two innings. It was

his first *live* pitching of the year. As he left, he told me pitchers today were not supposed to throw curves or sliders, only fastballs and change-ups; straight pitches. "*No way!*" he said. "I'm going to stand out there"—his voice rose in pitch—and throw straight pitches, and get my head knocked off? *No way!*"

When Dock came to the mound, Manny Sanguillen grounded out to third base on the first pitch. I heard Manny laugh as he came back to the bench. "Dock, he *curves* me!" he announced to everybody. "He no suppose to do that!"

3. Fans and the Militant

Dock Phillip Ellis, Jr., exercises his life in the pursuit of freedom. By freedom Dock means speaking his mind and doing what he needs to do without regard for consequence. This independence has not endeared him to fans. In the spring of 1975—to pick an example at random—a Pittsburgh newspaper printed a photograph of Dock running laps in Florida; his midriff was bare in the heat, and a dog was running after him. The photograph seems inoffensive, but someone in Pittsburgh took the trouble to cut it out of the paper, letter "No Good Black Rat" along the top, and mail it to Dock in Bradenton.

Of course when he makes the papers by screaming about the All Star game, or when he gets suspended, or when Commissioner Bowie Kuhn orders him to stop wearing hair curlers in uniform, then the hate mail piles up like slag. Some fans prefer their athletes docile, humble, grateful, clean-cut, and white.

So Dock—being proud, being black, and being his own man; possibly being eccentric—has more than his share of detractors. He can also count on some of the most devoted fans in the world, including most young black people in Pittsburgh, where he played his major league baseball until 1976.

All over the country, Dock is a roguish and spirited celebrity among black people, even among those indifferent to sports. *Jet* has so often printed photographs and news stories about Dock that it seems to have a Dock Ellis Division. *Ebony* has featured him. He is popular because he upsets white racists. He is popular like Muhammad Ali because he does what he pleases and gets away with it. He is popular because he is brave and stylish at the same time. He is also popular because he is loyal to black brothers and sisters everywhere, and spends his leisure in projects for black people—working at the rehabilitation of convicts, fighting sickle-cell anemia, and working with black youth. In these pursuits, he has avoided publicity. Readers of white sports pages know little of this side of him. He combines, in a way known only to himself, pizazz with dignity.

Much of the public does not *wish* to accord dignity to men who pitch, field, and hit baseballs for a living.

I remember June 8, 1974. Dock was scheduled to pitch against the San Francisco Giants at Candlestick Park. It was a Saturday afternoon game, and the sun was bright, but high winds from the Bay made it cold. Candlestick is the worst park in the major leagues. Made for football, it suffers a baseball diamond—awkwardly tucked on acres of green plastic—the way a circus horse tolerates a monkey. And no one comes to the games, not since Oakland arrived, across the Bay.

This Saturday was Camera Day. For nearly an hour before the game, fans crowded along the rails of the lower deck with Nikons and Polaroids, Leicas, Instamatics, Hasselblads, and antique box Brownies. The Giants strolled on the dirt at the edges of the field, offering themselves for photographs. One of them led a llama on a rein, another a pony, another a dog, another a camel. A young man not in uniform led a huge tiger. Ballplayers strayed close, but not too close, to the tiger.

Which were the animals, and which the athletes? At the zoo, every day is Camera Day. At Candlestick, only once a year do the visitors come close enough to the animal-athletes to fill camera frames with head and shoulders. The creatures behind the rail, camel or outfielder, gradually melted into each other.

Dock would never have taken part in such a show. In 1971—the year after his no-hitter, the year he started the All Star game for the National League, and won nineteen games—Dock was bannered in a Pittsburgh paper, ELLIS PROBABLY MOST UNPOPULAR BUC OF ALL TIME. Sportswriters all over the country had already censured his Bad Attitude. In Pittsburgh, he made people angriest when he refused to sign autographs. That's not exactly what he did, but that's what he was accused of.

Before every Sunday home game at Three Rivers Stadium, selected Pirate players hand out autographed photographs of themselves. In 1971, the players were sitting inside little cages to hand them out. The cage was there, presumably, to protect the players from the fans.

But the metaphor of the cage did not suit Dock. "I went up there and looked at it, so I said, 'I'm not going to be in a cage. I'm no monkey in a cage.' So they said, 'Well, if you don't do it, we're going to fine you.' I said, 'I don't care.'"

He cared enough to pay two sequential one-hundred-dollar fines.

Newspapers and television stations throbbed with indignation. One TV commentator, calling Dock "an egotistical pop-off," rehearsed earlier incidents and mounted to this climax: "Now the Pittsburgh prima donna is refusing to take part in . . . signing autographs in special booths before game time. . . . This past weekend my eleven-year-old son got the autographs of Bill Mazeroski and Bob Veale at just such a booth. He was thrilled. . . . By his action, Ellis has labeled himself as too big or too important to be bothered with the kids who hold him as something to look up to, with the fans who pay his salary. I intend to teach my son that that is not the behavior of a champion. . . ."

This one quote can stand in for a hundred others.

A year later, the Pirates changed the system.

Other players felt as Dock did, but did not speak out until he had provoked the usual abuse. Now the players sit at long tables while fans file by, and hand out photographs and sign yearbooks. A security guard stands by the table to protect them. Dock takes his turn.

Tomorrow he will sit at gate C. "I wish they would have me at gate B," he tells me. "I can sell more yearbooks there. Can I sell them! I must have sold at least fifty or seventy-five yearbooks. We don't sign *any*thing, but . . . let me see, what do we sign? . . . We sign *yearbooks*, that's all we sign is *yearbooks*. They'll throw a piece of paper at you, or a ball, and I'll say, 'We can't sign that. You've got to get a yearbook. Go get your yearbook!'" Dock is helping to support his employers.

"But you *are* handing out autographed pictures?" I ask him.

"Oh, yeah, I'll hand them out."

"Already signed?"

"We don't sign them. Somebody else signs them."

After I have digested this information, I ask Dock to elaborate.

"They tried to get us to sign the autographs beforehand. Like if I'm signing autographs tomorrow, I should have signed all those pictures two and a half weeks ago. But a lot of guys wouldn't do it, so they just said, 'Forget about it,' and they hired a girl to write the names. She does it *close!*"

With his own right hand, Dock Ellis signed more autographs than anyone else on the Pirates.

Before almost every game, in every park, Dock loiters along the box seats, walking from the outfield where he has been running, or from the bullpen where he has been throwing. People yell at him. He sees old friends. He chatters and makes new ones. Kids lean out, holding their pads and pencils. He will sign ten or twenty, move on, sign ten or twenty more. Frequently, he will make conversation with rapid questions: "Is that your sister? What you doing up so late? You go to school? Where? What's your daddy's name? Don't you like the *Pirates?*"

It takes forty minutes, some days, to walk from right field to the dugout.

Dock complains about the new parks. "You're just not as close to the fans as you used to be. If you don't have the fans, what're you doing out there playing ball?"

I ask him if he's aware—if ballplayers are aware—of old fans who have been coming to the park for fifty years, who watch the players change while the team remains the same.

"The DIEHARD fans," says Dock, with new heights of emphasis. "They sit out there in the rain, snow, everything. They won't *leave*, unless they've got bad health. They'll be *right there*. Today, I saw—" we were talking after a game with Cincinnati at Pittsburgh "—it was two guys, their wives. They said, 'Do you remember West Mound Street, Columbus?'" Dock spent two years at Columbus in the minor leagues. "I say, *'Yeah!'* That's where the ballpark was. I remembered the guy's voice, and I remember his wife from her glasses.

"Oh, you should have seen me out there today, after the game. I must have signed a hundred autographs. Of course I was trying to get close to that girl. I made sure I signed all their autographs, so they would *get away*! Of course they were Cincinnati fans, hundreds of them—they went *crazy*. She just happened to be blond."

All over the league there are fans that a ballplayer knows only at the ballpark. When you go into San Diego, you know you will see the fat woman on the third-base line whose husband arrives in the fifth inning. In Philadelphia there is a black family named Eustace always in left-field boxes. "Take Chicago. I have a lot of friends in Chicago, I don't know their names but I know their faces; I could see them anywhere and I'd know them. They got this Japanese family there. She takes pictures, and she took a picture, an *original* picture of me in curlers."

It must be unpleasant, though, to be yelled at by obnoxious fans.

Dock's face gets serious. This notion touches a principle he lives by. "The fan's *privilege* is to say what he wants to say. That's the same privilege I want, to say what I want to say and to do what I want to do."

Of course there is abuse from the fans. "Ellis, you stink!" "Hey, Ellis, crybaby!" "Ellis, where your curlers?" "You suck!"

Once in Chicago he had a quarrel going with the bleacher bums, as they called themselves. "I even had a grown man crying. I was just wolfing. I was getting on them *bad*. A man just shut up, and started crying. Then they apologize. They say, 'We didn't *mean* it.' I say, 'Well, okay, then, don't *say* nothing.'

"That particular time, that's when they *challenged* me to come to the bleacher bums' bar. They was the only ones they let *in*, there. Behind the scoreboard in Chicago. I stayed about an hour and a half. They all wanted to buy me drinks. They were just *amazed* that I came in there."

Not all the abuse is so open. Besides anonymous hate mail, there is the telephone.

"You get a lot of crank calls. You see in the papers, guys saying that people want to kill them? They've been trying to kill me ever since they started writing about me in the papers. If I *told* them, every time somebody called to say he was going to kill me, they'd have to put a man with me every day. They call me and say, 'If you peek your head above that dugout again, we're gonna blow it off!'"

Loitering along the rails signing autographs, Dock mostly talks to the kids. "Well, what's happening, my man?" When he gets abuse from white adults, sometimes he counterattacks through their children, setting young against old to make his point.

"Ellis, you stink! Ellis, if you're going to wear curlers, why don't you get out of baseball?"

Dock searches for the source of the taunts, and finds a pair of white adults with their children, sitting near the field, "I *charge* them. I run over to them, and say, 'What's your phone number? What's your address? Because I'm coming to dinner.'"

While the parents gawk, Dock levels his finger at a child and says, "Is that all right? Am I coming?"

"The child is excited anyway, by the fact of me being over there talking to them, because I'm a major league ballplayer. The kid is all happy about it and says, 'Yeah! Dock's coming to dinner.' The parents look like fools. What can the parents say? 'No?'"

And Dock telephones, and comes to dinner, and "They tell me they were booing only because they were going on what they'd read about me."

"How many dinners have you invited yourself to?"

"Three. It's a warm welcome. From there, we sort of become friends. They all still come to the ballpark. It just tickles the hell out of me! . . ."

Years ago, newspapers started to call Dock a "militant," short for "black militant." The word annoys him because it does not mean what it says.

In some ways, Dock is indeed a black militant, and wishes to be. When he was younger, during junior college, he read *Elijah Speaks*; in the minor leagues he went into "a heavy black thing" and isolated himself from whites. More relaxed now, he gets along as easily with whites as with blacks, travels in mixed company, and does not allow himself to be limited by any of the categories to which he belongs, "black," or "athlete," or "Californian." But he is alert to prejudice, he takes pride in his blackness, and he has been a particular friend to the young brothers on the team.

It irritates him that the press calls him "militant" when the term is inappropriate. When he complains about short beds or crowded airplanes, when he wears curlers or refuses to pitch relief, he is characterized as militant. If he complains about anything, he shows a Bad Attitude. If Dock Ellis returned a steak to the chef at Bonanza, complaining that it was too rare, a wire service would report: BLACK MILITANT DOCK ELLIS REFUSES STEAK. When Richie Zisk started screaming to the press about the way the Pirates were treating him, Dock—who regarded Zisk proudly as his pupil in public relations—called him a "white militant."

When someone calls Dock Ellis "militant" because he complains that his hotel bed is too short, he is calling him "an uppity nigger."

4. Hitting Batters

In the country of baseball, pitchers are always throwing baseballs at batters. Some pitchers are better known for it than others.

If the pitcher has acquired a certain reputation, the batter may have other matters on his mind besides his batting average, his ribbies, his slugging average, and his team's place in the standings. As Sandy Koufax has remarked, "Pitching is the art of instilling fear."

Dock Ellis is moderately famous for throwing at batters. On May 1, 1974, he tied a major league record by hitting three batters in a row. They were the first three batters up, in the first inning. They were Cincinnati Reds batters. Dock's control was just fine.

Four days earlier, I had seen him at a party in Pittsburgh. I wandered around, talking to various people. Dock's attorney and friend Tom Reich was there, shaking his head in disapproval of a plan of Dock's. I met Dock in the kitchen fixing a drink. I asked him with some awe, "Are you really going to hit every Cincinnati ballplayer Wednesday night?"

He returned the awe. "How you know that?" he said.

We must now consider the history, philosophy, and psychology of hitting batters.

In the challenge between mound and plate, which is the center of the game, a reputation can be as effective as an extra pitch. Dock: "The hitter will try to take *advantage* of you. Like if you are a pitcher who throws a lot of breaking balls, a lot of sliding fastballs, or if you pitch *away*, the hitter will have a tendency to lean across the plate. Quite naturally, if they know that this is your routine, they'll be trying to go *at* the ball, to get a better swing at it. They'll be moving up closer on the plate. Therefore, when you throw *in* on them, you don't throw to hit them, you throw to brush them back. That means: 'Give me some of the plate. Let me have my part, and you take yours! Get away! Give me some room to pitch with!'

"As far as *hitting* a batter, there are situations when it is called for, like sometimes a pitcher might intentionally or unintentionally hit a batter, or throw two balls near a hitter. The other team, to retaliate, will either knock someone down or hit a batter."

Not all pitchers will throw at batters. If you are a batter, you want *your* pitchers to throw at *their* hitters, to protect *you*.

Bob Veale was the Pirates' best pitcher for years. Between 1962 and 1972, he won a hundred and sixteen games. But he had a flaw. Gene Clines, a Pirate outfielder at the time, talked to me after Veale was traded to Boston: "He can throw the ball through a brick wall, but everybody knew that he was a *gentle* giant. If Veale would knock you down, it had to be a mistake. He didn't want to hurt anybody." Clines shook his head in bewildered melancholy. "Who's going to challenge him? Nobody on the *baseball field* is going to say, 'I'm going to go out and *get* Bob Veale.'... Take a left-handed hitter. Take Willie. They going to be going up to the plate, and digging in, knowing that Veale is *not* going to knock them down. ..." He shakes his head again, at the waste of it all.

"Blass was the same way." Steve Blass announced in 1973 that he would *not* throw at batters, even if management fined him for disobeying orders. "Now he was one guy that personally I really didn't like to play behind," Clines told me. "If they knock me down two or three times ... well, if *he* throws at a batter, he's gonna say, 'Watch out!' ... and I don't want that, because they never told *me* to watch out! They trying to knock my *head* off! Why go out there and play behind a guy that's not going to protect you?"

Manny Sanguillen: "I tell you about Veale. The only player Veale used to knock down was Willie McCovey. The only one. I was catching. Because McCovey hurt him so much." McCovey hurt Veale by hitting long balls off him. "You remember when McCovey had the operation here?" Manny, whose hands are as quick as the expressions on his face, jabs at his right knee. "Veale used to throw down at the knee!"

When Bruce Kison came up to the Pirates, Dock took to him immediately. Although Kison was six feet six inches and weighed only 155 pounds when he first reported (in the locker room, Dock says, when Kison breathed and filled his frail chest with air, he looked like a greyhound who could walk on his hind legs), he had acquired a reputation for hitting batters. If you hit batters, it is sensible to weigh 230 and look *mean* at all times.

"I was wild," says Bruce Kison, sprawled and smiling. "I've always had a reputation. . . . I have a fastball that runs *in*, on a right-handed hitter. In the minor leagues in one game I hit seven batters." Kison laughs, as if he were telling about a time in high school when he attempted a foolish escapade, like chaining a cow in the women's gym, and the cow kicked him, but nobody got hurt. "I was just completely wild. I hit three guys in a row. There were two outs. The manager came out of the dugout and said, 'Bruce, I know you're not trying to hit these guys, but we'll have the whole stands out on the field pretty soon!'

"The next guy up was a big catcher. *No*, he was an *outfielder*, but he came up to the plate with catcher's gear on. . . ."

I want to make sure I understand, "But you do, on occasion, throw at batters?"

"Certainly." Kison is no longer smiling. He sounds almost pedantic. "That is part of pitching."

A pitcher establishes his reputation early. Dock came up to Pittsburgh in 1968, and in 1969 was a regular starter. He quickly established himself as mean and strong. "Cepeda is the *biggest*," says Dock. So it was necessary for Dock to hit Cepeda. "He was trying to take *advantage* of me because I was a rookie. He was trying to *scare* me. I let him know, then, that I was not the type dude to fuck around with. It was a *big thing* because who would be hitting Cepeda? If you went for the biggest guy, it meant you would go for *anybody*. You weren't scared of *anybody*. I hit McCovey, and I really got *up* on McCovey that year. But he's not so big. Cepeda is the biggest. The rest of the season, from that point on, I had no trouble with the hitters. They were all *running*."

Sometimes one courts trouble, hitting batters.

In 1969, in Montreal, "I hit Mack Jones in the head, but I wasn't trying to hit him in the head. I was trying to hit him in the *side*.

"They had hit Clemente in the chest. So I said, 'The first batter up, I'm going to try to *kill* him. Mack Jones was the first batter. I threw at him. I missed him. I threw at him again. He ducked, and it hit him in the head. He came out to the mound, like he was coming at me." Players rushed out on the field. Enormous Dick Radatz, relief pitcher recently traded from Detroit to Montreal, ran in from the bullpen toward the mound. Dock addressed Radatz, "Hey, man, I'll turn you into a *piece . . .* of *. . . meat!*"

The umpire behind home plate looked as if he planned to interfere, possibly even to throw Dock out of the game. "But Clemente," Dock remembers, "he intervened, and he told the umpire, 'You leave Dock alone. The motherfucker's hit me twice! Don't mess with Dock!'"

On Wednesday night, May 1, 1974, the Reds were in Pittsburgh. Dock was starting against Cincinnati for the first time that year. As it developed, he was also starting against Cincinnati for the last time that year.

Beginning in spring training, among the palm trees and breezes and gas shortages of Bradenton on the Gulf Coast of Florida, Dock had planned to hit as many Cincinnati batters as possible, when he first pitched against them. He had told some of his teammates, but they were not sure he meant it. Dock loves to sell wolf tickets ("Wolf tickets? Some people are always selling them, some people are always buying them. . .") and the Pirate ball club had learned not always to take him literally.

Manny knew he meant it. At the regular team meeting before the game—the Pirates meet at the start of each series, to discuss the ball club they are about to engage—Dock said there was no need to go over Cincinnati batters, their strengths and weaknesses. "I'm just going to *mow* the lineup down," he said. To Manny (who later claimed to the press that he had never seen anybody so wild), Dock said, "Don't even give me no signal. Just try to catch the ball. If you can't catch it, forget it."

Taking his usual warm-up pitches, Dock noticed Pete Rose standing at one side of the batter's box, leaning on his bat, studying his delivery. On his next-to-last warm-up, Dock let fly at Rose and almost hit him.

A distant early warning.

In fact, he had considered not hitting Pete Rose at all. He and Rose are friends, but of course friendship, as the commissioner of baseball would insist, must never prevent even-handed treatment. No, Dock had considered not hitting Pete Rose because Rose would *take it so well*. He predicted that Rose, once hit, would make no acknowledgment of pain—no grimace, no rubbing the afflicted shoulder—but would run at top speed for first base, indicating clearly to his teammates that there was nothing to fear. "He's going to *charge* first base, and make it look like nothing." Having weighed the whole matter, Dock decided to hit him anyway.

It was a pleasant evening in Pittsburgh, the weather beginning to get warmer, perhaps 55 degrees, when Dock threw the first pitch. "The first pitch to Pete Rose was directed toward his head," as Dock expresses it, "not actually to *hit* him," but as "the *message*, to let him know that he was going to get hit. More or less to *press his lips*. I knew if I could get close to the head that I could get them in the body. Because they're looking to protect their head, they'll give me the body." The next pitch was behind him. "The next one, I hit him in the side."

Pete Rose's response was even more devastating than Dock had anticipated. He smiled. Then he picked the ball up, where it had fallen beside him, and gently, underhand, tossed it back to Dock. Then he lit for first as if trying out for the Olympics.

As Dock says, with huge approval, "You have to be *good*, to be a hot dog."

As Rose bent down to pick up the ball, he had exchanged a word with Joe Morgan who was batting next. Morgan and Rose are close friends, called "pepper and salt" by some of the ballplayers. Morgan taunted Rose, "He doesn't like you, anyway. You're a white guy."

Dock hit Morgan in the kidneys with his first pitch.

By this time, both benches were agog. It was Mayday on May Day. The Pirates realized that Dock was doing what he said he would do. The Reds were watching him do it. "I looked over on the bench, they were all with their eyes wide and their mouths wide open, like, 'I don't believe it!'

"The next batter was Driessen. I threw a ball to him. High inside. The next one, I hit him in the back."

Bases loaded, no outs. Tony Perez, Cincinnati first baseman, came to bat. He did not dig in. "There was no way I could hit him. He was *running*. The first one I threw behind him, over his head, up against the screen, but it came back off the glass, and they didn't advance. I threw behind him because he was backing up, but then he stepped in front of the ball. The next three pitches, he was *running*. . . . I walked him." A run came in. "The next hitter was Johnny Bench. I tried to deck him twice. I threw at his jaw, and he moved. I threw at the back of his head, and he moved."

With two balls and no strikes on Johnny Bench—eleven pitches gone: three hit batsmen, one walk, one run, and now two balls— Murtaugh approached the mound. "He came out as if to say, 'What's wrong? Can't find the plate?'" Dock was suspicious that his manager really knew what he was doing. "No," said Dock, "I must have Blass-itis." (It was genuine wildness—not throwing at batters—that had destroyed Steve Blass the year before.)

"He looked at me *hard*," Dock remembers. "He said, 'I'm going to bring another guy in.' So I just walked off the mound."

5. Rome Kicks Carthage Ass

In his May Day experiment, his point was not to hit batters; his point was to kick Cincinnati ass. Pittsburgh was *down*, in last place, lethargic and limp and lifeless. Cincinnati was fighting it out with Los Angeles, confident they would prevail in the end. And for Pittsburgh, Cincinnati was The Enemy.

In 1970, Cincinnati beat Pittsburgh in the Championship Series for the National League pennant. In 1971, with Cincinnati out of it, Pittsburgh took the pennant in a play-off with the Giants, then beat Baltimore in a seven-game Series. In 1972, three months before Roberto Clemente's death, Cincinnati beat Pittsburgh in the Championship Series, three games to two.

"Then," says Dock, "they go on TV and say the Pirates ain't nothing. . . ." Bruce Kison adds, "We got beat fairly in the score, but the *way* the Cincinnati ball club—the players sitting on the bench—were hollering and yelling at us like Little Leaguers. It left a bad taste in my mouth. I remember that. When I do go against Cincinnati, there's a little advantage."

In the winter of 1973–74, and at spring training, Dock began to feel that the Pirates had lost aggressiveness.

"Spring training had just begun, and I say, 'You are *scared* of Cincinnati.' That's what I told my teammates. 'You are *always* scared of Cincinnati.' I've watched us lose games against Cincinnati and it's *ridiculous*. I've pitched some good games at Cincinnati, but the majority I've lost because I feel like we weren't aggressive. Every time we play Cincinnati, the hitters are on their *ass*."

"Is that what the players are afraid of?" I asked.

"*Physically* afraid," said Dock. In 1970, '71, and '72, he says, the rest of the league was afraid of the Pirates. "They say, 'Here come the big bad Pirates. They're going to kick our ass!' Like they give up. That's what *our* team was starting to do. When Cincinnati showed up in spring training, I saw all the ballplayers doing the same thing. They were running over, talking, laughing, and hee-haw this and that.

"Cincinnati will bullshit with us and kick our ass and laugh at us. They're the only team that talk about us like a dog. *Whenever* we play that team, everybody *socializes* with them." In the past the roles had been reversed. "When *they* ran over to *us*, we knew they were afraid of us. When I saw *our* team doing it, right then I say, 'We gonna get *down*. We gonna *do* the *do*. I'm going to *hit* these motherfuckers.'"

When Dock had announced his intentions, he did not receive total support.

"Several of my teammates told me that they would not be there. When the shit went down, they would not be on the mound. Bob Robertson told me that. It really hurt me. I *believe* he was serious."

"Why?"

"Because this was benefiting him. He wasn't hitting but one oh two. Pitches coming up around his neck."

From time to time a batter who has been hit, or thrown at, will advance on the pitcher, the dugouts will empty, and there will be a baseball fight. Mostly, baseball fights are innocuous. But Dick McAuliffe once dislocated Tommy John's shoulder, and Campy Campaneris threw his bat at Lerrin LaGrow. But Dock thinks and plans. "I talked to other pitchers who have dealt with them on this level, one being Bob Gibson. He hits them *at random*! In fact, Pete Rose and Tommy Helms tried to whip Gibson, and Gibson got in *both* of them's stuff, in the dugout. He just went in and *got* them.

"I took everything into consideration, when I did what I did. Because I had to figure out who would fight us. Manpower per manpower, it had to be them. That's the *only* team that I could see would really try to *deal* with us. I was thinking of the physical ability of the two teams, and that was the only one that was comparable to us. The only one I could think of that was physically *next* was Philadelphia, and they wouldn't want to fight us. No way

95

would they want to fight us. If I hit twenty of them in a row, they ain't going to fight."

As Pittsburgh endured a dreary April, Dock's resolve intensified. "The team was down. I had to do something for the team. Everybody was complaining about this and that. We weren't winning, and every time I hear someone talk, he's talking about whose ass he's going to kick. On our own team, I mean." The defense was abominable—not just errors, but hits that could have been called errors, like the fly ball that drops in front of an outfielder, or the ground ball that an infielder seems unable to bend over for. Pitching and relief pitching were spotty, hitting streaky, with some of the team's best hitters looking sluggish and halfhearted. "So I said, 'I'm tired of hearing you talk of how *bad* everybody is. We're going to get the shit *on*.'"

One of the troubles with Pirate hitting was *fear*; batters were standing away from the plate; opposition pitchers were dusting them, moving them back, and then suckering them with balls on the outside corners. "My hitters weren't aggressive at the plate," Dock says. And a hitter would complain, "My pitcher wasn't protecting me," since retaliation is the best defense.

The game before Dock started against Cincinnati, a Houston relief pitcher hit Wilver Stargell on the head. If Dock needed fuel for his fire, this was sufficient. "They hit Willie in the head!" Willie Stargell and Dock were two of the tightest players on the club. "Houston had hit him on the head last year, and whether it was intentional or not, they hit him in the head again this year. And the next time I was to pitch was Cincinnati, and I had said *before* that I was going to get Cincinnati anyway, so everything more or less fell into line. I *could* have picked out the team that hit him on the head, but I took my anger out on the team that I felt *our* team was afraid of.

"Because now you had the team from the Western Division which was the champs, and the team from the Eastern Division which *should*'ve been the champs—both of them physically supposed to be strong, and on the field strengthwise as far as hitting goes. In the clubhouse I say, 'Well, we going to whip some ass.' It was a message I was trying to convey, to other teams throughout the league, to *leave my hitters alone*." It was also a message Dock intended for the Pittsburgh Pirates.

6. On Aggression

In the country of baseball, the citizens talk about aggression. Athletes talk about aggressiveness the way businessmen talk about profit margins. Many middle-class Americans—workers and clerks, teachers and small businessfolk—have problems dealing with their own aggression. Aggression is human and necessary, built into us by the craft and power of survival, but in our lives it can be destructive. We need to disguise it (as love or sexual drive, as gregariousness or good works) in order to live with it. Or we turn it inward on ourselves.

By definition, the athlete is someone who has few problems with his own aggression. Of course he must inherit and develop a skillful and powerful body, but the body is not enough. Everyone has known the superb athlete who never made it because he clutched; who would excel in practice or in warm-up, but in the heat of battle drop the ball. Recently a professional football team recruited a punter, from civilian life, who could hang the ball as high as the Goodyear blimp. But at a crucial moment of his first professional game, he fumbled a perfect pass from center, and his team lost. He turned in his uniform after the game.

The professional athlete—say he is twenty-seven—has been meeting challenges for twenty years. When he was seven and playing in the Little League finals, when he was seventeen and pitching for his high school in the state tournament, the tension was ultimate. There is no way that the World Series, when he is twenty-seven, is going to be a greater challenge than his high moments at the ages of seventeen and seven. Over the years, this athlete is self-selected as the man who is most able to summon and use his aggression.

Although a team is a collection of people with developed aggressiveness, something can happen collectively to depress this quality. A team, as a whole, can become depressed. Dock's insight—about Pirate players acting chummy with the Reds—diagnosed a team neurosis, an epidemic of fear and weakness. Making the diagnosis, the physician applies it to himself. In the lobby of the Pittsburgh Hilton, Dock Ellis bumps into Tony Perez, Cincinnati first baseman. Perez looks affable, says, "Hey, man, what's happening?" but Dock, pursuant to his designs, mutters something noncommittal and adopts his haughtiest expression.

Such a neurosis, the result of whatever trauma—maybe Clemente's death, maybe the stumbling loss to the Mets in 1973—can be cured, some think, by shock treatment.

It didn't work. Or, if it did, it took ten weeks for the electric current to shake up the synapses. Ten weeks largely spent losing ball games. When aggression fails, depression deepens.

"The only thing I did was prove that I was going to do what I said. I don't even think the guys on the team realize why I did it. That really hurt me. They couldn't understand why I did. That really hurt me, that they didn't understand. Even the guys that I did it for, they respect the fact that I did what I said I was going to do—but that's *all*. Like Stargell told me, he said that some of the brothers on the team might not like what I did. He said, 'It could hurt not only the brothers on this team, but the brothers throughout the league.'"

"So I said, 'Hey, Starge, I don't give a damn.' I know he'll tell me what he has on his mind. He was the only one that told me anything about it."

If you did it again, would you do it differently?

"I wouldn't do it again. My feelings was hurt."

Newspapers were full of stories about Dock's wildness, quoting Manny Sanguillen, "I never seen nobody so wild." Danny Murtaugh, told that it had been a deliberate act, summoned Dock and announced that he was fining him two hundred dollars. "Murtaugh pretended he didn't know anything about it," says Dock. "To this day, he's still looking for his two-hundred-dollar fine. Which is ridiculous." General Manager Joe Brown also called Dock in, and suggested that instead of mowing them down, Dock "beat them with the ball."

But, "that wasn't my mission," Dock says. "If that had been my mission, I wouldn't have thrown at anyone. I would have went out and pitched. My mission was to *hit* them. . . . I try now to relate back to the feeling I had when I was doing it. 'Ooh, buddy! Let me try to get him!' That's all I was into—how could I get him, how could I get him."

Around the ball club, nobody *talks* very much. The players chatter continuously—and no one more than Dock—but most of the chatter is light, a steady breeze of teasing, kidding, taking humorously the game and the combat which is deadly serious to them.

Before a game in which he will pitch, Ken Brett sees me early at the ball park, watching batting practice, infield, pepper, coaches hitting fungoes to the outfield. "What're you doing here so early?" he asks, cocky and fresh and friendly. Oh, I tell him, I love baseball; I'll watch anything, even calisthenics. Brett shrugs and smiles, "It's just a boys' game," he says. But when Murtaugh removes him for a pinch hitter, the Pirates losing by three runs early in the game, he stands in the dugout near his manager, staring at the wall behind Murtaugh's head, yelling, "Motherfucker! Motherfucker! Motherfucker! Motherfucker!"

Everybody, we can suppose, is really serious about his own career, and to varying degrees about his team and about winning and losing. But most of the time, it doesn't do to *act* too serious; acting serious is for baseball politicians, for organization men. So when Dock announced his intentions, nobody knew for sure if he was serious. When Bob Robertson said he wouldn't defend Dock, Dock couldn't be sure whether he meant it or not. When Willie Stargell told Dock that some of the brothers on the team hadn't appreciated the gesture, he didn't say who, or explain why—and Dock didn't ask him. Maybe asking would have seemed too much like caring. And anyway, after the event as before, nobody talked about it much.

Later in the season I asked Bruce Kison what he thought of Dock deliberately hitting the Cincinnati team.

Kison's face organized itself, and he said carefully, "Are you sure it was deliberate?" Kison speaks slowly, and seems to compose a sentence with all deliberate speed. When I assured him that the word had come from Dock, Kison's face relaxed. "I *loved* it!" he said. Then he remembered Dock's talk, beginning with spring training. "We didn't know if Dock was *sincere*. Most everybody was aware . . . but whether he was going to go *through* with it . . . ? Even after it happened, we could hardly believe it. . . . It was his idea that he was going to shake the ball club up. We were just going through the motions."

I told Manny Sanguillen what Stargell told Dock: that some of the brothers on the team were displeased.

Manny is incredulous. The muscles move in his ropy, mobile, sensible face, his forehead arches like a fly to center field. "Some of the Pittsburgh brothers? The Pittsburgh Pirates? The Pittsburgh *black brothers*?"

Gene Clines, sitting next to him, says, "I wouldn't doubt that at all."

Manny does not seem to hear Clines. His face becomes firm, even grim. He has decided he knows the reason anyone would disapprove, and it does not accord with his own set of values, which are firm and precise like his religion.

"Maybe the brother was scared," he says. "I'm not scared." Clearly, he speaks the truth. "Dock knock somebody down, other pitcher wait to knock you down too. Somebody get hurt. Me, I don't knock down too easy. I can move. I can move. When you throw the ball at me, sometime I catch it with my hand before it hit me." He gestures quickly, from the chair he is sitting in, and mimics a man snatching a baseball from a spot near his chin, like someone quick enough to catch houseflies in bare hands. He laughs. Then he is grim again. "I'm not scared," he says. "I know I'm going to die . . . and I know where I go when I die."

Two months after the incident, I chatted with Pete Rose about Dock.

"At first I just knew him playing baseball. I got to know him a little better at the All Star game in Detroit. His wife was there with my wife, and they were good people. We went out and ate, and he's a real good guy. Dock's just the type of guy—there's a lot of guys like him—he just wants to be left alone by reporters. When a reporter finds out that he wants to be left alone, then they really pester you.

"I like Dock as an individual, and he has a good arm. I can attest to that because he hit me the other day. He hit me right in the back and the damned thing hurt for about three days. I know he's still throwing good.

"A lot of small things happened to Dock. He's one of those fellows where controversy's always going to be around. Cassius Clay, he's the same way. In this life, you can't make people happy all the time. You go out of your way to sign a hundred autographs. Maybe one or two people you're not going to sign. They're going to go out and tell everybody you're an asshole."

"Had you heard rumors, before the game, that Dock was going to hit Cincinnati batters?"

"No. But when we left here we went to Houston, and the guys at Houston said that Dock said that he was going to hit the first five guys up." The Pirates had finished a series with Houston just before Cincinnati arrived May first. "I didn't quite understand that because Dock's not like that. If somebody hits me, they *hit* me, you know. That might ruin me. He had some heat on it, at my head. When you know a guy's throwing at you, that's not kosher, as we say. I didn't quite understand why he was doing that.

"You see, I like Dock. I like a guy that's an honest guy and I like a guy that if he wants to tell a guy to get fucked he'll tell them to get fucked. I like an honest guy, a guy that ain't scared to hide nothing. If Dock don't like you, he'll come right out and tell you. You've got to respect a guy like that. I don't necessarily like it when he says he's gonna hit the first five batters. You never know what might have happened. If we'd have known that before the game, there might have been a brawl."

Pete pauses, Pete makes a move. "But I'm *glad* he hit me because I don't usually get too many hits off him, and he just saved me an at-bat. He got me a run scored."

"What did the players say, when they found out for sure that Dock had hit them on purpose?"

"Some of the guys say because he's pissed off at the management. I don't know if he's pissed off at the management or not. It was before the trading deadline.

"He's got a good arm, he's a good bunter. I noticed that the last couple of years, he's made himself a good hitter. Learned to switch-hit, make a little contact on the ball. He works hard. He does his bats, and he's on the field on time, and things like that. Usually by himself, but there's a lot of guys like that. Some rookie comes along and stands by himself and nobody says anything, but because he's Dock Ellis, if he stands by himself in the outfield they say he's militant, they say he don't like nobody. He's always said hi to me, and asked how my little boy is."

Dock is crazy about Pete Rose's little boy. Pete takes his son to the ballpark for Cincinnati home games. "We've got a cage underneath the stadium. He can *hit*. He's four, now. I like to bring some of the opposing players and show them what a little work can do. Many of the other guys got little kids and they don't hit like my little boy. They don't work at it like he does. It's amazing. You'd be *amazed* to see how a four-year-old kid can hit. He's *aggressive*. I introduce him to all the players and he watches them. He goes to the games and he watches them on TV. It's a big thing for him."

A year earlier, when young Rose was three, Pete asked Dock under the stands to pitch to the boy. "He's just like his father," Dock says with admiration. "He *stands* just like him." Dock asked him where he'd like the pitch. "Get your shit over the plate," the boy said. "Get that damned shit over."

When I told Dock later that Pete Rose complained that his back hurt for days, Dock crowed with delight. "You see, that's the type of dude he is." It didn't hurt him at all, Dock claimed—but Pete knew that word would get back to Dock, and he was trying to psych him. When Dock heard that Pete said that he was *glad* that he was hit, because he doesn't bat too well against Dock, Dock roared with laughter. "He's lying. He's trying to *psych* me. That's what makes him so great. I hated for him to roll that ball back to me! He's a professional ballplayer."

I ask Dock: "Did you get any reaction from other Reds players?"

"No," he said. "Only Joe Morgan. He say he got a hundred and fifty dollars reward out, for any pitcher in the league that will hit me."

"Did you talk to Morgan about that?"

"I tell him, 'Hey, you're making a beautiful living playing baseball!'"

When aggression fails, depression deepens.

Dock didn't get a loss in the May Day game because the Pirates tied it up—but then they went on to lose the game anyway. They lost most of the time, early in 1974. As they found themelves flying to Cincinnati, six weeks into the season, the Pirates had won only fourteen games, and they had lost twenty-six, for an average of .350, and they rode well into last place. Dock was losing pitcher in twenty percent of the Pirate losses.

Dock was scheduled to pitch the first game at Cincinnati, four weeks and three days after May Day. But Murtaugh called him into the office and told him that he would miss two starts. He was giving Dock a rest, Murtaugh said, because of his "bad luck."

"I said okay. It was *child psychology*, and I didn't want to hear about it." Dock's "bad luck"—statistically speaking—was a one and five record and an ERA approaching five. He had never missed a turn in May. Possibly the Pirate management, knowing that Dock had deliberately hit the Reds six weeks before, feared that he would repeat himself, or that the Reds would retaliate against him.

(He would not have thrown at them. On the telephone I asked him if he was tempted to mow the lineup down again. "No No No," said Dock, like a trill on a piano; then, with delicacy and precision, "I—have—*delivered*—my—*message*.")

Then Murtaugh suggested that Dock might sit in the bullpen for a spell. Murtaugh explained that they "just wanted to take me out of the rotation. To let the winning pitchers—the ones that were hot—just keep pitching. They wanted to bring Bruce Kison in there. I listened to him *talk*. Well, the man has been successful with me, and I have been successful with him. I know for a fact that my fastball wasn't as lively as it had been before because they had hit many home runs off me, more on me this year already than they had all last year. I know for a fact my arm is not up to par. And so I just had to say, well, maybe the man is right."

But then the press picked up Murtaugh's words about the bullpen. "In Cincinnati, the sportswriters—and you can't pay too much attention to what they say—were bringing up the question of me taking Giusti's job, going short relief. And that would be cool. But I would definitely say they would have to pay me some *money* for it. To *relieve*, that would mean that I would have to cut out a lot of my extracurricular activities. It would break me down more or less as just being a *baseball* player. To be a short man, I'd have to be available everyday."

So Dock talked to reporters, and again Dock Ellis made the wire services, showed up in headlines in Boston and Little Rock. It was the annual flap, 1974 edition: ELLIS REFUSES BULLPEN. What he said, what he meant, and what he is quoted as saying interweave like braid. He would never relieve. He would relieve if they paid him. He would never relieve unless his team needed him desperately. A week later, I asked him what he really said.

"I said I would never go to the bullpen, and I would never pitch to a hitter, not even one inning, not even one pitch. I was misinterpreted, as far as the sports announcers go. They were saying that I would *never* pitch in the bullpen."

"But that's what you just said," I pointed out.

"But to be a member of a *team*, and a participant on this team, in order for them to *win*, if I have to pitch to a batter I *will* pitch to a batter. What I meant was I would never go to the *bullpen*, to be *in* the bullpen. But to pitch to a batter, or to win a game—Now if I was to go to the bullpen, then we'd have to talk about money. If I'm going to take an ace's job, then I want an ace's pay."

"What?"

"Giusti makes a hundred thousand dollars a year. I make seventy-two thousand five hundred."

After the newspaper flap, in order to save Danny Murtaugh's face, Dock threw some pitches in the bullpen in Cincinnati. He wasn't wearing a cup, which was his way of proving to himself that he had no intention of entering the game.

Who can say what lurks in all those hearts? Maybe he was removed from the rotation because Cincinnati management warned Pittsburgh management that matters could get out of hand. Maybe Danny Murtaugh, an expert at manipulation, was applying some shock treatment, attempting to psych Dock into greater effort and concentration.

Maybe Murtaugh really felt that Dock might develop into a relief pitcher, especially since Giusti was having problems. Or maybe he felt that if Dock underwent the humiliation of being long man—the reliever who enters the game early when the game is already lost—his hurt pride would restore his fastball. If Murtaugh really expected him to do relief, then Dock outpsyched the psycher, with his blasts to the press. (The Manual of Aggression includes a chapter on the use of public relations.) He pitched no relief in 1974.

7. Sparky Steps on Spanky's Foot

The general depression continued in the first half of the season.

On July 10, the Pirates were still in last place. Dock started against Atlanta, gave up three runs immediately, and was relieved in the first inning. It was his eighth loss against three wins.

Cincinnati came to town, the first visit since May first, for a five-game series including two double-headers. The Enemy won four straight, giving Pittsburgh another five-game losing streak. Reuss, Rooker, Demery, and Brett all started and lost. Brett, whose pitching so far had been the brightest moment of the season, gave up a three-run homer to Tony Perez in the first inning of the first game of Sunday's double-header, July 14, and pitched immaculate ball thereafter, but lost three to two.

The Pirates were undergoing humiliation. They were down, they were low, and they felt mean. Cincinnati was riding high in pursuit of the Dodgers, a pursuit that most of the players, as far back as July, believed would succeed. But Cincinnati was also aware that on its last visit, it had been thrown at. The mob was restless. It was Bastille Day. In Bruce Kison, who started the second game, the mob had a leader.

Kison is a reliever and a spot starter, with an uneven record and great courage. He comes from the side, frequently, powerful against right-handed batters, and finds himself in trouble with left-handers. Spotty though his record may be—he ended the regular season, in 1974, with nine wins and eight losses—he rises to the challenge. Everyone remembers his performance as a twenty-year-old rookie in the 1971 World Series. At the end of the 1974 season, he rose from a series of setbacks to beat the Cardinals in St. Louis—the game that put Pittsburgh ahead—and next pitched a three-hitter to beat the Mets and sustain the Pirates in their push toward the Eastern Division title. In the third game of the Championship Series with Los Angeles, Kison gave up four hits and no runs to the team with the best record in baseball.

Pitching to right-handed batters, Kison throws a fastball that breaks up and in. Pitching against the right-handed Cincinnati

Reds—George Foster, Johnny Bench, Tony Perez, Dave Concepcion—he kept his fastball riding toward chins. When Concepcion went down from a fastball in the second inning, the umpire behind the plate, Ed Sudol, walked to the mound and warned Kison not to throw at batters. Both benches emptied. There were words. Nothing happened.

When Sudol returned behind the plate, Kison resumed the task of pitching to Concepcion. As he put it later, "I assumed that he would be looking for a pitch down the middle, after I had been warned; so I jammed him."

In the fourth when Kison batted, Cincinnati pitcher Jack Billingham hit him with the first pitch. When the ball knocked Kison's helmet off, everyone assumed that Billingham had hit him on the head. Actually, the ball hit Kison on the left arm and bounced to his shoulder, "one of the few places where I have any meat," and thence to the bill of his helmet. "It didn't cause any pain. I lay on the ground, and I was kind of dazed. I thought he called it a foul ball. 'You've got to be kidding.' By that time, everything had started. Sanguillen was out there, but I never even *knew* he was out there, he was so fast getting out there. I wasn't mad. I wasn't mad at all. Obviously, whether I was doing it on purpose or not, a lot of their hitters had gone down."

Manny was mad. Quick as a hummingbird, with his perpetual smile, Manny Sanguillen is the most affable and the most volatile of the Pirates. He is also, probably, the best boxer. "That smile," says Dock, "that smile is *dangerous*."

Around the mound, and at various points in the infield, the rival players confronted each other. Sparky Anderson, manager of the Reds, and Spanky Kirkpatrick, Pittsburgh utility man, were standing next to each other. At first, Dock watched from the base line. "Sparky stepped on Spanky's foot. Then Spanky pushed him. That's what they say started it." Andy Kosco, Cincinnati reserve, threw the first punch, after seeing Spanky push Sparky. Unlike most fights in the country of baseball, this fight had some fighting in it. It lasted twenty minutes.

"All hell broke loose," says Dock, grinning. "Manny was hitting everyone. It was ridiculous, he's so quick. If one of our players got in the way, *he* got hit. He didn't hit them in the face or nothing, but he was *swinging*. He was body punching, just like a boxer. When I saw him, I wanted to do it too.

"That's when it started around third base. I was trying to get to Billingham because it was him that hit Kison. The umpire was pushing me. Fists started flying, and you didn't know what was happening. I would see three Cincinnati ballplayers on a Pirate, which at that time was [Daryl] Patterson, and somebody had him by the hair. So I started to step on the dude's hand, but I was afraid to step on Patterson's head. Stargell just took his thumb back, and bent it. That took care of that.

"Before Borbon grabbed Patterson by the hair, Patterson had him in an armlock, and was going to pound his head in. Ain't no way he could have got away from Patterson. And the Cincinnati ballplayers was begging him to let him go. I could hear them, 'Please let him get up. Let him get up. Let him get up.' And I looked, I saw Daryl had him, so I saw there wasn't any need to be dealing with that. When I looked back over there, Borbon had him by the hair. When Patterson let him go, Borbon *bit* him. Bit him bad. Like an animal bite. He had to have a tetanus shot. Pulled part of his skin away, with his teeth."

The Pirates went on to score, after the dust had cleared, and after Sparky and Spanky, together with Andy Kosco, had been thrown out of the game. Kison pitched well, and left the game in the seventh inning only when a blister puffed out on his middle finger like a button mushroom. Giusti was perfect in relief, and the Pirates won, two to one. The Pirates agreed that they had won the fight as well as the ball game.

Aggression Returns. Son of Aggression. Aggression Rides Again.

Later that Sunday night, over drinks all over the city, the ballplayers rehashed the fight. The team that had been dour and sullen transformed itself.

In the dugout the next day, everyone was cheerful and ebullient.

No one could forget it. Every detail was repeated with care and detailed attention. There are events we wish would never stop, which we repeat endlessly, like television—doing over and over again a stunning moment: the deflected forward pass which wins a championship, the first step on the moon. Even in the press club, where the reporters drink gin and eat sandwiches free, everyone was cheerful, everyone repeated what *he* saw, what *he* heard someone say.

And everyone apportioning credit or blame asserts that this skirmish, in the war between the clubs, began not when Kison decked Bench on a curve ball in the first inning, but on May first when Dock knocked down three in a row. "It was *bound* to happen," Jack Billingham said, in the clubhouse after the game; "Dock hit three in a row. . . ."

In Cincinnati in August, the Pirates took two out of three, and there were no fights. From Bastille Day on the Pirates averaged a little better than two out of three. First, they won eight straight games, beginning with Dock's complete game victory over Houston the next day. Then, after losing one, they won nine of eleven. From last place they rose steadily, with little vacillation, until they passed St. Louis and Philadelphia to take first place on August 27. They were kicking ass.

PROSEBALL:

Sports, Stories, and Style

Baseball accounts not only for poetry but also for the best prose. It provides background to fiction by Ring Lardner, Bernard Malamud, Robert Coover, Mark Harris, and Philip Roth—and fiction forms only a portion of proseball's lineup. Proseball is Roger Kahn, Roger Angell, and John Updike (once, at least), whose metaphors and images glorify the game. At the other extreme, it is the *as-told-to* (*att*), in which a journalist ghosts a ballplayer's autobiography, often with a splendid disregard for history in the service of myth. It is newspaper writing, which ranges from the clichés of the ordinary journalist—full of literary "stanzas" and "cantos"—to the inventions of Red Smith, Jimmy Cannon, or Tom Boswell. It is also the tape-recorder book, the edited recollections of old ballplayers, most notably Lawrence Ritter's collection of interviews with old-timers, *The Glory of Their Times*. It is also the uncommon excellence of certain former players who write as well as they played: Pat Jordan is best, who never made the majors; the relief pitcher Jim Brosnan wrote two good books. Then there was Jim Bouton. . . .

Neither football nor basketball provokes nearly so much writing. In football there are a couple of goodish books. Although basketball is fashionable among intellectuals, it makes little happen in literature; there is Bill Russell's *Second Wind*, *att* Taylor Branch; there is David Halberstam's *The Breaks of the Game*. Both sports encourage penis-envy prose: in football, envy of meat violence, splintered bone, and cleat marks on the eyeball; in basketball, gray-boy envy of black cool.

Proseball's lineup is deep, the players innumerable, and the success . . . ? Well, in proseball as in baseball we undergo the splendor of triumph and the agony of defeat. But even when the style is ghastly, full of booted grounders and bases on balls, often the stories are magnificent.

In a sense, baseball literature began its wide ranging some time ago, for the game is old; or at least its name is old. In "The Poet's Game," I quoted a poem published in 1744. The *Oxford English Dictionary* doesn't catch up with baseball until later; its first citation occurs in a passage from *Northanger Abbey* (1818), which John Fowles uses as an epigraph for his article comparing cricket and baseball: "It was not very wonderful that Catherine should prefer cricket, baseball, riding on horseback, and running about the country at the age of fourteen, to books . . ." At no time in the early years is it quite clear what "baseball" refers to. It *seems* safe to assume reference to something played with a ball; it *seems* safe to assume bases. . . . Probably the game resembled an English children's game called rounders.

When I went up to Oxford in 1951—a Brooklyn Dodger fan fortunately missing a certain play-off game; and missing my first World Series—English undergraduates asked me to explain baseball almost as frequently as they asked me to distinguish between Republicans and Democrats. When I began an account of baseball's rules and conventions, I was always interrupted by apparent comprehension: "It's only rounders!"

Alas, baseball more or less *is* rounders. Our legend that a Civil War general named Abner Doubleday invented baseball is a nationalist lie. The game Jane Austen referred to was the common ancestor to baseball, to rounders, and doubtless to other sports that have failed to evolve into the present—mighty ruins along the lines of Neanderthal man. (Cricket existed before 1818; its remote ancestry is surely similar to the ancestry of baseball and rounders.) In the American colonies, children played One Old Cat, as well as Two and Three Cat—the name varied with the number of players—which resembled the ancestor game. During the Revolution, American troops played something they called "base ball" or "town ball." In 1786 a Princeton student wrote in his diary about playing "baste ball." During the Civil War troops from all over the country playing together acted to regularize the rules.

Literary folk from England, doubtless under Jane Austen's influence, have been charitable to the American game. Rupert Brooke described it as played at Harvard College in 1913, writing in *Letters from America* that "baseball is a good game to watch, and in outline easy to understand, as it is merely glorified rounders." P. G. Wodehouse became a fan and wrote a frequently anthologized story called "The Pitcher and Plutocrat." It seems less predictable that William Empson, at Kenyon College in 1950, captained a team in softball called The Ambiguities for games in the Ohio summer evenings; opposition was supplied by L. C. Knights' The Explorers. Empson recalls John Crowe Ransom's suggestion that *Some Versions of Pastoral* might have included a section of games; we can doubt that he was considering football.

Maybe the *echt* baseball book remains the *as-told-to*, or the *att* for short, like Christy Mathewson's instructive book on the art of pitching, splendidly titled *Pitching in a Pinch*, which was ghost-written by a baseball reporter named John Wheeler and originally appeared in 1912. The book was reprinted in 1977, allowing us to read witticisms reattributed in the years since. Here the young Mathewson, whose catcher that day was Jack Warner, discovers the only weakness of the great batter Honus Wagner:

Wagner loomed up at the bat in a pinch, and I could not remember what Warner had said about his flaw. I walked out of the box to confer with the catcher.

"What's his 'groove,' Jack?" I asked him.

"A base on balls," replied Warner, without cracking a smile.

That's always been Wagner's "groove."

It has been observed throughout proseball's history that certain batters were best pitched where they could not touch the ball.

In the matter of quotation marks, Mathewson/Wheeler reveals the influence of Henry James, an American writer not known to have demonstrated an interest in baseball. For that matter, Mathewson/Wheeler does not truly show great interest in prose style. *Pitching in a Pinch*, like most examples of the *att*, supplies the anecdote while it withholds sentence, image, and metaphor.

For sentences, images, and metaphors, we may observe the High Belletristic Tradition, which doubtless borrows from the best newspaper writing of a hundred years but which in its purest form began with John Updike's visit to Fenway Park, September 28, 1960, to observe Ted Williams's last at-bat; this tradition represents the fan's view from the stands, glorified by good prose, rather than the newspaper reporter's locker-room expertise. Its finest practitioner is Roger Angell with his uncommon intelligence and fine prose style. But he is not alone.

There is also Roger Kahn, best known for *The Boys of Summer*, which takes its title from a line by Dylan Thomas, "I see the boys of summer in their ruin." (Kahn had trouble persuading his publishers to accept his title; they thought it sounded homosexual.) Although Kahn is High Belletristic, he began writing as a sports reporter, and this book combines a journalist's interviews with fan's lyrical reminiscences. Kahn's ruined boys are the Brooklyn Dodgers of the 1950s; there is a good deal of nostalgia and ruin in baseball prose, as recollection remains at the center of things, underscoring the essential conservatism of baseball writing. Writers are concerned not only to preserve a tintype of the past but also to keep baseball's present in a living tintype. Doubtless this latter endeavor is foredoomed by the tycoons who own the teams—and the newer tycoons who play the game—but foredoomed endeavors appeal to literary quixotes.

What saves baseball, perhaps, is its peripheries. The game is too often confused with the major leagues—or even with Joe Garagiola and the Game of the Week. But baseball is college and Little League, high school and vacant lot and American Legion and class A. In his baseball book after *The Boys of Summer*, called *A Season in the Sun*, Roger Kahn spends a summer touching down at the four corners of the baseball world. He begins in the late spring with a wonderful visit to Wally Moon, who played for the Cardinals and the Dodgers in the fifties and sixties and who was now coaching baseball for John Brown University in Siloam Springs, Arkansas. This return visit to the baseball world continues the spirit of *The Boys*, but moves itself from old coach to young players: every single player on the John Brown University team believed that he had a chance to make the majors.

In the next chapter, Kahn jets to Walter O'Malley's office at Dodger Stadium in Los Angeles, where the tycoon, sitting in the center of baseball's richest franchise, glowers at a groundsman watering center field with a hose while a $600,000 sprinkler system went unused. From the affluence of Chavez Ravine, Kahn's *Season* slopes downward to Houston with its then-hapless Astros, more than thirty million dollars in debt; to Double-A ball in Pittsfield, Massachusetts; to Artie Wilson, car salesman who starred in his heyday in the Negro leagues, coming up to the majors only at the end of his career; then to another ruined boy, Early Wynn, intelligent and aggressive gentleman who pitched during four decades in the major leagues and won three hundred games; to the island of Puerto Rico, where the population is baseball crazy; to Bill Veeck, baseball-crazy genius, at the time owner of the Chicago White Sox; and finally to the bright sun of autumn, to the Apollo of the 1976 World Series—the great John Bench.

If there are places Kahn does not travel—a rookie league, where Methodist boys from Oklahoma meet stars of the Brooklyn streets, hipper than Mick Jagger, and where former cane cutters from the Dominican Republic meet Arizona State communications majors; or a triple-A team, where players wait nightly for a message—still, *A Season in the Sun* is thick with the old virtues of baseball prose. Kahn is a master of baseball anecdote, with a sweet ear for the cadence of baseball talk.

Here is Dixie Walker coaching Steve Yeager: "Think opposite field, Steve, think other way. They're going to give you outside sliders, Steve." Here is Early Wynn talking about throwing at batters: "Why should I worry about hitters? Do they worry about me? Do you ever find a hitter crying because he's hit a line drive to the box? My job is getting hitters out. If I don't get them out, I lose. I don't like losing a ball game any more than a salesman likes losing a sale. I've got a right to knock down anybody holding a bat." Then Kahn repeats a story: A reporter asked Wynn, "Suppose it was your own mother?" And Wynn replied, after the briefest pause, "Mother was a pretty good curve-ball hitter."

Then Kahn carries the story one step further, the way the best comedian makes you laugh again after you think you have finished laughing: " . . . at Yankee Stadium I saw Wynn brush his own son." Wynn's son was named Joe Early, and he was visiting Yankee Stadium when his father threw batting practice one day. "Joe Early hit a long line drive to left center. The next pitch, at the cheekbone, sent Joe Early diving to the ground. 'You shouldn't crowd me,' Wynn said. . . ."

People who aren't fans always ask me—when I repeat a story I took from Roger Kahn or quote an image remembered from Roger Angell, or when I describe with enthusiasm a play I remember from forty years ago—"What *is* it about baseball?"

If one weren't so tired of the remark, one could repeat Louis Armstrong's *bon mot*; but too many people have used it as an excuse for not thinking. It is true that no one who is now indifferent to the game will suddenly take pleasure in it just because I come up with a reason for the pleasure that the rest of us take. But . . . reading baseball prose, often I understand a necessity underlying the love of the game, a necessity that is doubtless one of my own. Like other sports, baseball provides harmless dissipation for those of us who need on occasion to be less serious or ambitious—or depressed—than we usually are. This function is related to the formal appeal: baseball as pastoral, in John Crowe Ransom's notion, baseball as grid. In Robert Coover's novel, *The Universal Baseball Association*, his obsessive hero constructs a life out of the imaginary league with its structure determined by the die's cast. A firm grid of baseball statistics holds together a life otherwise drifting into chaos. If not statistics, there is the daily ritual of games and box scores, strategy and planning, guessing and second-guessing: baseball provides structure for the structureless.

For example: Art Hill is a Detroit Tiger fan who published *I Don't Care If I Ever Come Back* in 1980. The book is a pleasant rumination, the journal of a season or two. Reading this mild man's book about his hobby, we come to know and enjoy the writer (possibly wishing he did not love E. B. White quite so much) and suddenly, after we register many references to alcoholism and other darknesses, we realize that the hobby is *desperate*—as a focus of attention outside the self, the sports-obsession keeps the world manageable.

For Art Hill and for many others, baseball is a clean well-lighted place that keeps terrors away until dawn.

With so much poetry and prose about baseball, it is inevitable that many anthologies collect baseball writing. These books provide an overview of the genre.

Baseball Diamonds is the craziest; it is also serious and entertaining. Edited by Kevin Kerrane and Richard Grossinger, this collection bears the subtitle "Tales, Traces, Visions, and Voodoo from a Native American Rite." It includes Angell, Kahn, and Pat Jordan; it includes Willie Morris, Philip Roth, Roy Blount, Jack Kerouac.

. . . It contains experimental prose writers and Black Mountain poets, counterculture jocks whose alienation from American culture stops short of baseball: Robert Kelly, Tom Clark, Lewis Warsh, Gilbert Sorrentino. . . . Baseball's uniqueness brings these writers together with the president of Yale University, A. Bartlett Giamatti—self-proclaimed baseball maniac.

There is also *A Baseball Album*, edited by Gerald Secor Couzens, which does not know what it is; sometimes it is an anthology reprinting remarkable and out-of-the-way pieces of prose; sometimes it interrupts itself to list trivia on some baseball subject or other. Yet I require the book for its best pieces: John Fowles on cricket and baseball, Dr. Harold Seymour on "How Baseball Began," a wonderful old-man's reminiscence of "How I Pitched the First Curve" by William Otter Cummings, and a terrifying profile of dying Ty Cobb by Al Stump.

This Ty Cobb article is also collected in Charles Einstein's *The Baseball Reader*, which is the baseball anthology to buy if you can only buy one. Cobb was a great player and everyone in baseball hated him, and he hated everyone in baseball. In the rich old dying man, Al Stump observes the enduring characteristics: Cobb was vicious, energetic, brave, arrogant, unforgiving, angry, unyielding—extreme in every human characteristic except for the gentle ones.

The Baseball Reader reprints selections from the same editor's series of *Fireside Books of Baseball*, and it adds new pieces. Einstein includes fiction, excerpts from a biography, newspaper reporting, articles from magazines, even one transcription from radio commentary. Well edited, the book continually surprises: H. L. Mencken, Grantland Rice, Kenneth Patchen, "Casey at the Bat." . . . This book includes the famous John Updike piece on Ted Williams's last day at Fenway Park; playing his last game with the Boston Red Sox, in his last at-bat, Williams hit a home run. "It was in the books while it was in the sky," says Updike.

Brandt ran back to the deepest corner of the outfield grass, the ball descended beyond his reach and struck in the crotch where the bullpen met the wall, bounced chunkily, and vanished.

Like a feather caught in a vortex, Williams ran around the square of bases at the center of our beseeching screaming. He ran as he always ran out home runs—hurriedly, unsmiling, head down, as if our praise were a storm of rain to get out of. He didn't tip his cap. Though we thumped, wept, and chanted "We want Ted" for minutes after he hid in the dugout, he did not come back. Our noise for some seconds passed beyond excitement into a kind of immense open anguish, a wailing, a cry to be saved. But immortality is nontransferable. The papers said that the other players, and even the umpires on the field, begged him to come out and acknowledge us in some way, but he refused. Gods do not answer letters.

My goodness: "Gods do not answer letters." The prose is so velvety one surrenders assent, ignoring Infantile Polytheism.

And one should never think that such worship is unacceptable to the God in question, or to deities from rival teams, like Joe DiMaggio (evidence supplied below). A few years back, a sportswriter, a prose fan as well as the fan of aged left-fielders, approached the portly graying figure of Ted Williams as he instructed Red Sox farmhands at the batting cage in spring training. The reporter summoned courage—Williams does not hold the moral character of the journalist's profession in high regard—and asked him what he thought of Updike's article. The Splendid Splinter paused a moment, searched for a word, and delivered the laconic line: "It has the mystique."

And in this collection, valuably, we follow the same day from a different vantage. Updike writes from the stands, the fan who creates a myth to believe in. On the other hand, a reporter for *Sport*, Ed Lynn, hangs around the locker room and reports in workmanlike prose about a baseball player who is talented, sullen, complex, and definitely lower than the angels. Lynn's metaphors are less enthralling, his Ted Williams more credible.

Maybe I am right that Updike's small article started the high belletristic tradition; maybe I am wrong. But I will not admit the possibility of error (nor will many contradict me) when I claim that Roger Angell writes the best prose of all baseball writers of all time.

At present writing, he is accumulating in the pages of the *New Yorker* his fourth collection of baseball essays. They began with *The Summer Game*, which came out with Kahn's *The Boys of Summer* in 1972. (It was the season of seasons. When Pat Jordan brought out his marvelous—and relatively obscure—essays on baseball a little later, he was belittled by a me-too title, *Suitors of Spring*.) *The Summer Game* was marvelous, but, if anything, Angell has improved. In *The Summer Game*, Angell remained largely in the stands, describing the green mural as innings transpired before him—descriptions that blended the welcome repetitions of the game with its sudden minute varieties of action. He described a painting (a strange one, with moving figures) that carried its own light with it. In *Five Seasons*, which followed, he described baseball as if it were sculpture that changes as you perceive it by walking around it or as the day's light moves over stone from pink dawn through white noon to yellow twilight.

He has come to write, not only observing the game itself, as the sport's most articulate *fan*, but also observing the work of those on the sidelines—owner, ex-player, roving scout—and he writes of lawsuits and commissioners, players' unions and free agents, lockouts and the designated hitter and nighttime World Series TV spectaculars; he writes of Howard Cosell and Bowie Kuhn.

Still, the *best* of Angell renders the game on the field. He loves to describe Luis Tiant's pitching motion, stylist on stylist; on page forty of *Five Seasons* we hear, in Angell's best note-taking manner:

> Stands on hill like sunstruck archaeologist at Knossos. Regards ruins. Studies sun. Studies landscape. Looks at artifact in hand. Wonders: Keep this potsherd or throw it away? Does Smithsonian want it? Hmm. Prepares to throw it away. Pauses. Sudd. Discovers *writing* on object. Hmm. Possibly Linear B inscript.? Sighs. Throws. Wipes face. Repeats whole thing.

And on page two hundred-and-ninety-five, in the same book, challenged again by stupified observation, he takes another tack; same pitcher, different *tack*:

His repertoire begins with an exaggerated mid-windup pivot, during which he turns his back on the batter and seems to examine the infield directly behind the mound for signs of crabgrass. With men on bases, his stretch consists of a succession of minute downward waggles and pauses of the glove, and a menacing sidewise, slit-eyed, Valentino-like gaze over his shoulder at the base runner. The full flower of his art, however, comes during the actual delivery, which is executed with a perfect variety show of accompanying gestures and impersonations. I had begun to take notes during my recent observations of the Cuban Garrick, and now, as he set down the Reds with only minimal interruptions (including one balk call, in the fourth), I arrived at some tentative codifications. The basic Tiant repertoire seems to include:

(1) Call the Osteopath: In midpitch, the man suffers an agonizing seizure in the central cervical regions, which he attempts to fight off with a sharp backward twist of the head.

(2) Out of the Woodshed: Just before releasing the ball, he steps over a raised sill and simultaneously ducks his head to avoid conking it on the low doorframe.

(3) The Runaway Taxi: Before the pivot, he sees a vehicle bearing down on him at top speed, and pulls back his entire upper body just in time to avoid a nasty accident.

(4) Falling Off the Fence: An attack of vertigo nearly causes him to topple over backward on the mound. Strongly suggests a careless dude on the top rung of the corral.

(5) The Slipper-Kick: In the midpitch, he surprisingly decides to get rid of his left shoe.

(6) The Low-Flying Plane (a subtle development and amalgam of 1, 3, and 4, above): While he is pivoting, an F-105 buzzes the ball park, passing over the infield from the third-base to the first-base side at a height of eighty feet. He follows it all the way with his eyes.

I forgot to mention that, in the course of rendering and advocating, Angell from time to time is extremely funny.

Five Seasons is a fans' notes from 1972 through 1976, five early seasons, five ongoing seasons, five specimens of the World Series featuring the 1975 epic between Reds and Red Sox. Angell describes extraordinary things with humor and vigor, but he excels at rendering the game's ordinary moments—a normal July in an undistinguished year—and stops action like a good sports photograph, freezing for the perpetual album of memory not a dramatic moment but a typical one. Baseball's *echt* moment is typical or ordinary; those who cherish the game cherish repeated scenes, and Angell is Ben Jonson to the diamond's humors.

In *Five Seasons* there's a long chapter on a baseball scout, Ray Scarborough; there's a brilliant section about Steve Blass, the Pittsburgh pitcher who suddenly and unaccountably lost the control that had been his meal ticket, never to retrieve it. Because Blass is an agreeable, humorous, likeable man—as well as (formerly) an excellent pitcher—he has been the subject of articles by baseball's best prose writers; Roger Kahn and Pat Jordan, as well as Roger Angell, have had their say on Steve Blass. Angell's has been the most considerable say.

Angell's prose is graceful and pleasant, with never a misstep, never cliché or corn or overstatement or pomposity. What a pleasure it is to read him, like the pleasure of watching effortless fielding around second base: Angell can *pick it.* And his overall essay construction, as well as the dance of syntax and the proportion of analogies, makes for our pleasure. He paces his paragraphs with a perfection of tact—up and down, slow and fast, back and forth— leading readers lightly, giving them just enough of each subject to leave them wanting more. I watch his essayistic trickery with admiration and despair, much as a beer league softball pitcher might observe Luis Tiant.

When Angell comes to the subject of baseball's owners, and the imperatives of television—to Howard Cosell and Bowie Kuhn— anger replaces his usual good humor: he defends the game against the Forces of Hype. Cosell is obnoxious; his broadcasts interrupt baseball for show business, with dictionary words thoroughly misused; but Bowie Kuhn is more dangerous, who fronts for corporate greed at the expense of an American institution. Angell leaves us a vision of Commissioner Kuhn at his work of con: sitting upright, falsely cheerful, freezing to death in a suitcoat at an October TV World Series night game, which is played under wintry stars— against the game's nature—to score high ratings for advertisers.

Criticism of baseball's enemies form a rightful part of this book because Angell's prose and vision serve the game. But the *plupart* of *Five Seasons* is grandly positive. For instance, the book begins with a superb meditation on "The Ball," which concludes with a passage of mad genius:

> I don't think anyone can watch many baseball games without becoming aware of the fact that the ball, for all its immense energy and unpredictability, very rarely escapes the control of the players. It is released again and again—pitched and caught, struck along the ground or sent high in the air—but almost always, almost instantly, it is recaptured and returned to control and safety and harmlessness. Nothing is altered, nothing has been allowed to happen. This orderliness and constraint are among the prime attractions of the sport; a handful of men, we discover, can police a great green country, forestalling unimaginable disasters. A slovenly, error-filled game can sometimes be exciting, but it never seems serious, and is thus never truly satisfying, for the metaphor of safety—of danger subdued by skill and courage—has been lost. Too much civilization, however, is deadly—in this game, a deadly bore. A deeper need is stifled. The ball looks impetuous and dangerous, but we perceive that in fact it lives in a slow, guarded world of order, vigilance, and rules. Nothing can ever happen here. And then once again the ball is pitched—sent on its quick, planned errand. The bat flashes, there is a new, louder sound, and suddenly we see the ball streaking wild through the air and then bounding along distant and untouched in the sweet green grass. We leap up, thousands of us, and shout for its joyful flight—free, set free, free at last.

Late Innings makes Angell's third collection, and I suppose he receives the loving cup for Writer of the Best Baseball Sentences, the third time in a row—and we might as well retire the trophy. He doesn't invent the most dazzling image nor concoct the zaniest juxtapositions; he constructs a model of informal prose, a model with virtues wholly independent of its subject—accurate, humane, particular, thoughtful, observant, modest, skillful, and appropriate. Never does he strain for a figure of speech or contort himself into a stance. His prose has the ease that comes from hard work and good editing. When Tom Seaver, elegant and powerful pitcher, was traded from the New York Mets in 1977 after a dispute over his contract, Angell's ruminations included a mimetic rendering of Seaver's delivery; of all the parts of the game that Angell describes, probably he describes pitching the best, from Luis Tiant's eccentricities to Tom Seaver's classicism:

> . . . the motionless assessing pause on the hill while the sign is delivered, the easy, rocking shift of weight under the back leg, the upraised arms, and then the left shoulder coming forward as the whole body drives forward and drops suddenly downward—down so low that the right knee scrapes the sloping dirt of the mound—in an immense thrusting stride, and the right arm coming over blurrily and still flailing, even as the ball, the famous fast ball, flashes across the plate, chest-high on the batter and already past his low, late swing.

The visual accuracy, together with the kinetic rhythm of the long sentence, allow Angell to fly past the game's moment to broader considerations.

> Our national preoccupation with the images and performances of great athletes is not a simple matter. The obsessive intensity with which we watch their beautiful movements, their careless energy, their noisy, narcissistic joy in their own accomplishments is remarkably close to the emotions we feel when we observe very young children at play. While their games last, we smile with pleasure—but not for long, not forever. Rising from the park bench at last, we look at our watch and begin to gather up the scattered toys. . . .
>
> Off the field, Tom Seaver is not a child, of course, but an articulate and outspoken young man, with strong opinions about the business side of baseball, the relations between professional athletes and their employers, and the nuances of his difficult profession. . . .

Although Angell cherishes a childlike awe of these athletes, he is also "an articulate and outspoken [middle-aged] man, with strong opinions." He takes a moral view, and he delights when he can identify ethical superiority with a winning team:

> . . . those of us who are on the scene and in the clubhouses remarked again and again on the poise and generosity and intelligence of the

players on both teams. This was a refreshing and surprising change from the demeanor of several more famous clubs and better-paid athletes in recent Octobers.

Angell covers not only major league games on the field. In *Late Innings*, he chronicles the efforts of women sportswriters to gain access to locker rooms. He also tells how, early in the 1981 season, he attended a college game in the company of Smokey Joe Wood, ninety-one years old, who won thirty-one games as a right-handed pitcher for the Boston Red Sox in 1912. His companion allows Angell to imagine a past he was not alive for—in 1912, Wood pitched a famous 1–0 game defeating Walter "Big Train" Johnson and the Washington Senators—while the two men watch a pair of fine young pitchers go twelve innings, and Frank Viola of St. John's beat Yale's Ron Darling 1–0. Angell concludes:

> Somebody will probably tell Ron Darling that Smokey Joe Wood was at the game that afternoon and saw him pitch eleven scoreless no-hit innings against St. John's, and some day—perhaps years from now, when he, too, may possibly be a celebrated major league strike-out artist—it may occur to him that his heartbreaking 0–1 loss in May 1981 and Walter Johnson's 0–1 loss at Fenway Park in September 1912 are now woven together into the fabric of baseball.

In August of 1981, while the major leagues were out on strike, Angell followed a baseball-crazy pitcher in a semipro league in Vermont. No money. No great talent. Great love for the game.

Money is a theme in almost all baseball books, whether or not they are written in prose. *Late Innings* begins with an account of the compensation given free agents in the salary wars promulgated by baseball's owners. For that matter, when people wrote about baseball in 1908, they talked about money, and writers in the twenties noted that Babe Ruth's salary was greater than the President's—prompting the Babe's famous response that he had the better year—and in the 1950s writers attacked and defended Ted Williams's annual $100,000.

Roger Angell follows the figures with appropriate curiosity and does not allow himself a flap about it. He only regrets, as we all must, that great players will no longer be associated with one team and city. There was something touching about the notion that Ted Williams was Boston's as Joe DiMaggio was New York's. But Rod Carew, in a world of free agency, could not remain the property of Minneapolis. No longer will marriages endure between ballplayers and cities, but the best athletes will float like Reggie Jackson on promiscuous contracts from place to place. . . .

Of course, these contracts are social levelers, spreading the riches; if these athletes have sense and luck, they will never pump gas again but will enjoy fortunes of dimensions formerly associated with cornering the North American fur market or arranging for rebates from railroads. With these fortunes, in the old time, ballplayers' daughters would have married into European nobility, their sons would have bought seats in the Senate. The money, for the American imagination, only makes these athletes more mythic —Babe Ruth and Howard Hughes together. . . .

Baseball fiction has always used the game's mythic propensities— sometimes realism multiplied by exaggeration, as in Bernard Malamud and Ring Lardner; sometimes fabulous entirely, as in Philip Roth's *Great American Novel*. His baseball names are as wonderful as real baseball names; one hardly notices that Gil Gamesh is the game's first Sumerian superstar. Then there is the mythic exaltation of the obsessive statistician, as in Robert Coover's *Universal Baseball Association*.

Every year there are rookie baseball novels, most of them sent down to the pulp machine by June. Few survive as well as Mark Harris's real/funny/mythic series about Henry Wiggen, left-handed pitcher for the New York Mammoths. In 1953 came *The Southpaw* (later, *Bang the Drum Slowly* and *A Ticket for a Seamstitch*), and, more than twenty years later, Harris published *It Looked Like Forever*, which is not so much about baseball as it is about aging. But then *Bang the Drum Slowly* was not so much about baseball as it was about dying.

It is the strength of these novels—it is the strength of much baseball writing—that Mark Harris uses material we would normally associate with pennant races, box scores, and sports pages, and by his skill and compassion turns whatever he touches into our ordinary, universal lives.

It Looks Like Forever begins with losses. Henry Wiggen at thirty-nine has lost his fastball, and last season he won only three ball games. When his old manager drops dead on the golf course, Wiggen attends the funeral expecting to be named his successor as manager of the New York Mammoths. But he loses again. At the end of the first chapter, Wiggen is passed over for manager and released as ballplayer.

Naturally, the news shocks and annoys Henry; like all athletes, he thinks he is good for another year or two. It also upsets his daughter Hilary because she has never seen him play ball. Hilary is spoiled, a youngest child who screams bloody murder when she wants something she does not have. A problem child, she is perhaps a problem in this novel, where we see rather a lot of her. Still, she allows Henry to extend his acquaintance. Hilary's psychiatrist is a Dr. Schiff, in whose office Henry meets a tennis star named Suzanne Winograd. Since Dr. Schiff, like Ms. Winograd, is an attractive young woman, Henry's life of erotic temptation receives further extension. Rather, it is extended in one direction while it is retracted in another. If baseball is disloyal to the aging Henry Wiggen, so is Henry's body, for as soon as he is dismissed from baseball his prostate gland acts up.

Enough of plot—my indiscretions come from the beginning of this book, which covers considerable variety of place and action: Japanese expansion baseball, a horse farm, a young woman who wishes to freeze Henry's body for one hundred and twenty-five years, Friday Night Baseball and other television hype—and too little of the game itself, which is a pity. Harris's accounts of baseball games and pennant races have always been exciting, the compelling background of action against which his characters have played out their moral quotidian dramas.

Only one false note in Harris's diamond Arcadia has ever bothered me, and that is the sound of the shepherds' song lyrics. When I saw the good film of *Bang the Drum Slowly*, it disturbed me that the coaches all sounded like Rodney Dangerfield. Reading this novel, I think I understand where this language comes from. The father of the Henry Wiggen novels is clearly Ring Lardner, with Mark Twain a reasonable grandfather. But Damon Runyon is the disreputable uncle whose accents invade the dugout, in the *Saturday Evening Post* argot of guys and dolls. One of the chief mannerisms of this style is the intermixture of the genteel or literary cliché with nonstandard English. In this novel, double negatives spread like dandelions, yet Henry says things like, "My daughter Hilary will be extremely grief-stricken if she does not get to see me play again." "Grief-stricken" is pure Nathan Detroit.

But Harris rises above his mannerisms. He remains entertaining, using the pop character of Henry Wiggen to make intelligent moral generalities, which most tellingly include Henry Wiggen's own self-doubts. At the beginning of an old-timers' game, Henry hears, in a moment of silence, something he has never heard before: "It was the sound of many people crying. It all been crying since Dutch's funeral. And who were they crying for? Was Patricia [clubowner] crying for Dutch? Were all these people crying for Big Ben Scotland [eldest of old-timers] and me? No, I was crying for my self. Everybody was crying for them self." When Henry proceeds to violate the game's spirit by throwing fastballs past old men, we participate in his shame. When it works, this writing can create a community by which we withstand or understand disaster—Vietnam, the meaningless death of the young, an enlarged prostate gland, and, in an earlier work of art, the failure of Mudville's Casey.

This is something that sportswriting can do: it can take the popular and find the universal in it, take the boys' game and find in it ambition and failure, success and aging. When you hazard such notions to a bunch of baseball reporters, they will make noises like violins at you—but they mock themselves and you, for they know it is true. It is easy to be corny about baseball. . . . And sometimes corn—Casey, Grantland Rice—is universal, serious corn. With a subject ostensibly light, writers feel free to play, to vary tone, to lose themselves happily to metaphor, to laugh, and even to lament. In baseball's diamond and numerical order, writers find a grid against which to set phenomena of time and the times—like aging, like the behavior of owners. In baseball history writers find connection with the past that most Americans, most of the time, ignore or deny.

Of course newspaper sportswriting is mostly terrible—and of course it is usually the best writing in the paper.

Mostly it is terrible by being tired, ordinary, trite, and false. The clichés vary from decade to decade. Old clichés revisited acquire charm, but in day-to-day reading they deaden the mind. And worse than the clichés, perhaps, is the false energy of much newspaper sportswriting—macho wise-guy cynicism that sneers, winks, and then pokes the reader in the ass.

Still, there is more decent prose about baseball on the American sports page than the editorial page supplies on the subjects of debt and SALT. Red Smith is dead, but there were Red Smiths before him and there are Red Smiths still alive. Maybe the best baseball writer of the moment, among the daily newspaper set, is Peter Gammons of the *Boston Globe*. Gammons is strictly a newspaper writer; he left the *Globe* for a year at *Sports Illustrated* and wasted his talent. He writes a lively, tight, observant game story, and he excels at the background column. All year he writes a lengthy Sunday baseball gossip column. His prose is witty, authoritative, and factual, strong with moral judgment, like an eighteenth-century historian's. Only the readers of the *Globe* know how good he is.

I call him "maybe the best" because I have one other candidate. If I did not live in the *Globe*'s neighborhood, maybe I could subscribe to the *Washington Post*, for the other great newspaper baseball writer of our day is Tom Boswell. Unlike Gammons, Boswell is inconsistent, and, unlike Gammons, he is not limited to newsprint. He has collected his magazine features into a book, *How Life Imitates the World Series*.

Writers are as different as athletes, who perpetually divide themselves into those who feel natural in what they do, born to their skills, and those who pride themselves on the difficulty with which they learned those skills. The first type climbed from the crib with the eye's ability to discriminate the spin of a slider. The second, instead, listened to an American Legion coach explain the virtues of the batting stance; at the hundred-thousandth repetition, the lesson was learned. I think of the old Dodger George "Shotgun" Shuba, who told Roger Kahn how he practiced his swing six hundred times a day off-season, "47,200 swings every winter. . . ." Thus, there are writers who boast about the number of their revisions, and others who brag about their facility. No doubt we are never quite what we think we are or what we pretend to be; no doubt the difference represents character more than history; yet character differences are as appreciable as history. Roger Angell writes as if he practiced, Thomas Boswell as if he didn't, Peter Gammons as if he didn't need to.

Boswell is pure scholar of the sport as well as a naturally gifted prose writer. He is quick to write a game story on a word processor, and when he slows down to write for a monthly magazine, his pace remains lively. He is adept at the startling image. When he observes a crucial out of the 1980 World Series—a pop foul, escaped from the Philadelphia catcher's glove, was caught by the aging and omnicompetent first baseman Pete Rose—he describes it: "Rose's lizard tongue of a mitt...flicked out...to gobble the fly."

Such a dexterous small chain of metaphor, developed with no clang of symbols, would go unremarked in the briefest exchange between the least of Shakespeare's royal advisors. But in American prose of our moment, it is an extended purple patch. I am grateful to Tom Boswell, and to the sports pages, for watering the garden of metaphor in a dry time. The sports section is the only place in the paper where we are likely to find an image more complex than an adjective accompanied by a noun, or a metaphor neither inadvertant nor trite nor mixed. Of course, we may permit ourselves a reservation in our pleasure: a metaphor-hating society allows metaphor on the sports pages only because it considers the subject trivial.

It is also true that Boswell displays some of the faults that sports-writers are prone to. When his imagination provides no hungry lizard-glove, he sometimes strains visibly for color. His paragraphs turn nervous and punchy, we hear the wisecrack and the portentous one-liner, we hear the Muzak of pretense: "Everywhere you look there are un-self-conscious rituals, rites of passage, and a gentle, unhurried symbolism." Perhaps Boswell hurries his symbolism?

But I am ungrateful. . . . Boswell has a good ear for baseball speech, like Roger Kahn's. He listens, and he brings it back for us: "Reporters, for instance, are called 'green flies at the show' because, in the minors, buzzing green flies are a symbol of annoyance, while 'the show' is the universal busher's term for the majors." Or: "Once outfielder Carlos Lopez disabled two Baltimore mates in a week in collisions while chasing flies. Fellow Oriole outfielder Ken Single-ton, asked for a general evaluation of Lopez as a center-fielder, said simply, 'He'll never take me alive.'"

And Boswell repeats a ballplayer's trope, which compares a large and enthusiastic manager (Frank Howard) to an amphetamine pill: "We call him the 300-pound greenie. . . ."

Boswell is also a fine storyteller, reporting on a sport gloriously afflicted by the anecdote. He repeats a story about Thurman Mun-son, Yankee catcher killed in a plane crash at the age of thirty-two, which the Oriole shortstop Mark (called "Blade"—a skinny fel-low) Belanger told him:

"Munson always said, 'How's it going, kid?' to rookies, and 'How's the family?' to the veterans when we come to the plate," Belanger said. "One day, I got furious and said, 'Thurman, we all know what you're doing. You're trying to distract me and I'm hitting .190. Just leave me the hell alone. Just shut up when I'm up here or I'll hit you with the bat.'

"He got this terrible hurt expression and said, 'Jeez, Blade, I didn't know you felt that strongly. I swear I'll never say another word to you.'"

On his next at-bat, Belanger was all ready to swing when the high-pitched penetrating voice behind him said, "How's the family, Blade?"

Or there is another, about fame I suppose:

Returning from a USO tour of Korea, Marilyn Monroe told her husband, Joe DiMaggio, then retired, "Oh, Joe, it was wonderful. You never heard such cheers."

"Yes, I have," was DiMaggio's clipped reply. . . .

If Boswell is a student of this game, myopic in observation—"no sport rewards its devotees in such direct proportion to the quality of their attention"—his professor is none other than Earl Weaver. Now Weaver, although a pedagogue, is not a bookish man. I cherish a story I read some place. When he faced retirement in 1982, ready to quit after sixteen years as contemporary baseball's model manager, he confronted the prospect with equanimity. He told a reporter, "Being retired is boring if you have to sit down and read a book . . . but if you can go to Vegas or play golf every day, and go to the track every night . . ." Boswell covered Weaver's Orioles for his Washington paper, and Weaver is a shrewd fellow who cannot resist revealing his shrewdness. When Boswell gives us a source for some insight, it is often Earl Weaver; there is the Weaver Theory of the Big Inning, Weaver on pitchers, and the Weaver adage, "This ain't a football game; we do this every day."

A few paragraphs ago, I mentioned the name of Red Smith. His final column for the *New York Times*, called "Writing Less—and Better?," appeared in January of 1982. The tone was faintly elegiac, as it announced his decision to cut back from four to three columns a week. Alas, the cutback was considerably more severe because Walter W. Smith, seventy-six years old, died of heart failure four days later. No longer would he practice the literary form of the sports column that in his hands resembled the form of the sonnet. Late in the year of his death appeared two volumes collecting hundreds of his columns; that's something.

Smith himself edited *To Absent Friends*, one hundred and seventy-nine columns of tribute and elegy for men and horses. Dave Anderson, who succeeded Smith at the *Times*, edited *The Red Smith Reader* after his friend's death. "If you blindfolded yourself," he says in his introduction, "reached into Red Smith's files, and yanked out one hundred and thirty columns, *any* one hundred and thirty columns, you would have a good collection." In the absence of other criteria, Anderson mostly chose columns "about big names, big events, big issues," starting with those from the *St. Louis Star* in 1934, through the *Philadelphia Record*, the *New York Herald Tribune*, four years with a syndicate, and ending with eleven years on the *New York Times*. During some of these years, Smith wrote seven columns a week; he figured he had written more than ten thousand columns.

Red Smith was a good reporter, a brilliant phrase-maker, on occasion a fierce moralist—and he was best at telling a story. No writer assembles the brief anecdote with more (necessarily invisible) skill. Often his narrative art is one of omission; the teller gives *just enough* of the tale, so that one word leaps forth to do the work of a hundred. Smith excelled in the anecdotal lead that illustrated character or introduced theme:

> Society Kid Hogan was hurrying through the Illinois Central pedestrian tunnel under Michigan Avenue on June 9, 1930, when a man in the crowd put a gun to the head of Jake Lingle, a grafting crime reporter, and it went *blooie*.
> The Kid kept right on walking.
> "Why?" the Law asked him later.
> "The last train was leaving for the racetrack," he said reasonably.

Ah, the art of the adverb! . . . Here's a story from a column about Grantland Rice:

> When Warren Harding was President he asked Granny down to Washington for a round of golf and Granny invited his friend, Ring Lardner.
> "This is an unexpected pleasure, Mr. Lardner," Harding said as they hacked around. "I only knew Granny was coming. How did you happen to make it, too?"

"I want to be ambassador to Greece," Lardner said.

"Greece?" said the President. "Why Greece?"

"Because," Lardner said, "my wife doesn't like Great Neck."

Rice, Red's friend and model, turns up frequently in these pages:

Grantland Rice, the prince of sportswriters, used to do a weekly radio interview with some sporting figures. Frequently, in the interest of spontaneity, he would type out questions and answers in advance. One night his guest was Babe Ruth.

"Well, you know, Granny," the Babe read in response to a question, "Duke Ellington said the Battle of Waterloo was won on the playing fields of Elkton."

"Babe," Granny said after the show, "Duke Ellington for the Duke of Wellington I can understand. But how did you ever read Eton as Elkton? . . ."

"I married my first wife there," Babe said. . . .

One could go on quoting, and quoting, and quoting . . .

These two Red Smith anthologies repeat each other a bit—not so much in the whole columns as in illustrative anecdotes or favorite lines—and *The Red Smith Reader* is the better book because its tone is more varied. *To Absent Friends* ululates one continual elegy, and the obituary note is not always Red Smith's best. A generous and affectionate man, he is given to eulogy (the word *great* uses itself up fast) and sometimes to sentimental distortion; we learn soon enough that the word "guy," as in "class guy," signals disorder in the sincerity-neurons. Sometimes we suffer the portentous coda—the sportswriter's devil—as in a column about Red Rolfe, which ends with the brief graph:

Class was something Red had no trouble recognizing. He saw it every morning when he shaved.

But there are also, in this book as well as the *Reader*, wonderful writing and superb anecdotage.

Smith's best columns describe horse playing (he cautions us to avoid "horse racing") and boxing, with baseball a close third; he writes wonderfully as a participant, about fishing—fishing with friends, with sons and grandsons. (The world of his column is almost exclusively male.) He dislikes basketball, never writes of hockey in these pages, and takes potshots at track and field; he repeats once or twice his contention that, if the Creator had wanted humans to race, he would have given them four legs. . . . Almost every column is funny enough for laughter. Many are also serious.

When he is serious, he is never pompous or self-important. "I've always tried to remember," he told Jerome Holtzman in an interview, "that sports isn't Armageddon. These are just little games that little boys can play, and it really isn't important to the future of civilization whether the Athletics or Browns win." Elsewhere he quotes one of his heroes, his old *Tribune* editor Stanley Woodward, who warned against "Godding up these ballplayers." I suspect it's useful, if you are as widely praised as Red Smith was, to keep modest sentiments in front of your eyes, like samplers hanging on the wall. We must not "God up" sportswriters either. . . . But I permit myself to take newspaper sportswriting more seriously than he does—and perhaps more seriously than I take sports.

Within the pastoral of the sporting world, general human concerns become isolated and magnified—the triumph, et cetera; youth, aging, and death, tra-la-la . . . —so that, if we have moral ideas in our heads, we have a scene to which we can apply them. Thus Smith permits us to enjoy his rare invective as it dissects the vanity of George Steinbrenner (usually "George III"), the hype of Howard Cosell, the hypocrisy of Bowie Kuhn and Avery Brundage. He becomes angriest when sport is unwilling to look beyond itself—as when the National Football League refused to cancel games after Kennedy's assassination; as when the Munich Olympics took the murder of Israeli athletes as a political intrusion on amateurism.

Maybe moral ideas become *most* useful in the ethics of prose style. Smith is a writer before he is a sportsman. "Writing is easy," he said. "I just open a vein and bleed."

Honest sportswriting helps keep prose alive. For a culture survives not only through its high-art embodiments; we study beauty less from paintings at the Metropolitan than from daily encounters with an honestly designed beer bottle. Thus, it is commonplace to observe—as I observed a few pages back—that the best newspaper writing occurs in the sports pages: editorials bore, news stories deaden, features inflate, reviews pontificate—but sports pages remain lively, play with words (when Mr. and Mrs. Zatopek both won gold medals at the 1952 Olympics, Smith called his column, "Czech and Double Czech"), and seek out figures of speech.

Metaphor is a way of thinking available to everyone, which has nothing to do with elitist education, except that elitist education seems to discourage it. Shakespeare could talk no other way, and the pit had no trouble following him—but modern intellectuals do. It's true that some living cultures encourage metaphorical speech —the Irish, American blacks—but the Department of English is by and large suspicious and hostile; colorful speech gets confused with language that has designs on us—like the rhetoric of politics and advertising—and intellectuals resist metaphor for fear of being taken in. Textbooks quoting poems for American classrooms footnote metaphors, translating them into the clichés of flat prose.

So the sports column—as Red Smith did it—becomes a wildlife refuge for metaphor and all liveliness, where language lives and breathes. Smith calls the Olympics "this conclave of gristle," providing us with synecdoche. . . . But surely hyperbole is his favorite trope; for instance, he writes about the place of bicycle racing in French culture: "an army from Mars could invade France, the government could fall, and even the recipe for sauce Béarnaise could be lost, but if it happened during the Tour de France nobody would notice." He loves the bright figure and continually quotes the *bons mots* of others: "Lefty Grove was a pitcher who, in the classic words of Bugs Baer, 'could throw a lamb chop past a wolf.'"

I do not mean to say that Red Smith's language is equal to Shakespeare's. I mean to say that because we take daily English lessons from, oh, Alexander Haig, Ronald Reagan, and the authors of beer ads, we need Red Smith and his progeny.

When I call most sportswriting "terrible," maybe I exaggerate. Maybe I don't. For an example of the dreary ordinary product, I am content to use Murray Chass, another *New York Times* reporter, with his sad affectations of vitality: "Guidry could probably knock out an alligator in his hometown bayous. Guidry's slight frame lends an aura of mystery to his ability to throw a ball so fast." An aura of mystery . . . ? This prose wins the inevitability contest: "Because of a quirk in scheduling, the Yankees would not play their arch-rivals, the Red Sox, until June 19, but then would clash . . ." Quirk. Arch-rival. Clash. Urp.

Of course, bad writing about sports does not confine itself to newspapers. In 1934 the St. Louis Cardinals, known as the Gashouse Gang for their disreputable appearance, came from behind to win the National League pennant, then won the World Series. Frankie Frisch was player-manager, Pepper Martin was third baseman, Leo Durocher was shortstop, Ducky Joe Medwick played left field, and Dizzy and Paul Dean were pitching. If Roger Kahn in *The Boys of Summer* could recount the exploits of a Dodger team twenty years back, why could not Robert E. Hood go back a little further to write *The Gashouse Gang*?

Well . . . because he lacks a talent for writing prose. This man has a genius for cliché: cars move "at a snail's pace" when winter has deposited "a blanket of snow." Reading *The Gashouse Gang* is painful, like reading two hundred old newspapers in a row. We undergo numerous weather reports: "In St. Louis the temperature was falling and the *Post Dispatch* 'weather bird' predicted four degrees above zero for the night." We undergo headline-scanning historical background: "The *Morro Castle*, a luxury liner, caught fire off the coast of New Jersey. One hundred and thirty-five people lost their lives in the burning ship. Two hundred thousand textile workers walked off their jobs in a nationwide strike. Bruno Richard Hauptmann was arrested. . . ." We even suffer the following juxtaposition, sports history at its most fatuous: "The Nazis were cutting deep into France and charging through Holland and Belgium. The British were retreating to a dark rendezvous at Dunkirk. And in Brooklyn, the Dodgers had just dropped four straight games. . . ."

And if we needed a book on Japanese baseball, we did not need *The Chrysanthemum and the Bat*, by Robert Whiting. This book includes enough facts about *besuboru* to fill two books. Alas, the facts give no pleasure in the telling. Robert Whiting is nobody's writer, and this book is ill written and ill assembled. Whiting organizes a chapter—on managers, say—by presenting us first with Generalized Manager of a Generalized Ball Club on a Generalized Day, which includes a Generalized Interview with a Generalized Owner. After this orgy of probability, we hear a few anecdotes about real managers, one following another in assembly-line prose, with the shuffled sound of three-by-five cards audible in the background.

For the baseball addict who does not cherish the game of words, the book provides an ensemble of curiosities. For instance:

During the season, games appear nightly on Japanese television, nationwide, but only for one hour and twenty-six minutes; at that moment—be the bases loaded, be the count three and two, be Sadaharu Oh at bat—the set winks off.

When we hear about the regimen of Japanese spring training, every moment accounted for from early morning until late at night, we realize that in contrast American spring training resembles six weeks at the Fontainebleau.

In Japan, the foreign superstars have been not only American but also Chinese (Oh is Chinese, from Taiwan), Korean, and Hawaiian; and one great pitcher of the past was White Russian. The Japanese apparently look down on the foreigners—but are prepared to cheer when they win a game for the home team. The parallels to the American game are obvious, with our Panamanians, Cubans, other Latins—and one Samoan.

When we look at baseball of the American past, its racial provinciality lends it a distance, from our present, as great as Japan's.

G. H. Fleming's innovative *The Unforgettable Season* provides a history of the National League season in 1908, when John McGraw's Giants spent the summer struggling with the Chicago Cubs and the Pittsburgh Pirates. Fleming's innovation is not to write this book but to collect it. *The Unforgettable Season* is pasted up from newspaper accounts of the moment. "I have read every relevant issue of New York's twelve daily newspapers of 1908," says Professor Fleming, "as well as the Brooklyn *Eagle*, three daily papers from Philadelphia, two from Boston, two from Pittsburgh, three from Chicago, two from St. Louis, and one from Cincinnati, along with the two baseball weeklies, the *Sporting News* and *Sporting Life*. . . ." No one who reads the book will doubt his proud assertion. It is history by collage, documentary narrative, a rapid series of clipped voices, continually varied, that explore a single historical context, interrupted only by Fleming's brackets to identify a name, an outlived practice, or a piece of slang.

The author-editor is professor of English at the University of New Orleans, and his earlier titles include *Rosetti and the Pre-Raphaelite Brotherhood*. Strangely, the photographs in *The Unforgettable Season* look contemporary; so many white ballplayers now *look* Victorian; with their shaggy heads and voluminous mustaches, they look like the players in the photographs of ancient times that illustrate baseball's coffee-table books—those doughty rows of young men who stare at the camera as if it were a rookie fireballer named Rube. Their eyes are heavy and alert like Cap Anson's eyes; they stand poised with hands on knees to run, catch, stop, whirl, and throw with sullen precision. Their bodies look like those wooden figures painters use instead of human models, with ellipsoidal shoulders, upper arms, forearms, trunks, and thighs.

If baseball writing helps to preserve metaphor, it also provides Americans with something that they lack more profoundly than they lack colorful prose—which is to say history, or the historical sense, or the sense that people decades or centuries back were both like and unlike us. In *The Unforgettable Season*, although we notably lack Panamanians and Samoans not to mention American blacks, hundreds of sentences might have come from this morning's paper—especially complaints about commericalism in the game.

There were remarkable events in 1908, and *The Unforgettable Season* has lived on in baseball anecdote, without Mr. Fleming's help, especially in recollections of poor "Merkle's bonehead play. . . ."

Whatever the prose style—be there quirks and clashes or macho bruises—the *story* sits at the center. Let me end this arbitrary tour of baseball (mostly baseball) prose writing with a little garland of stories clipped from my reading.

The umpire Tom Gorman tells stories to Jerome Holtzman in an *att* called *Three and Two!* He tells us that Yogi Berra liked to chat with opposing players as they came to bat, distracting them with genial questions. He did the same with umpires. One day when Berra had been unusually talkative, he came to bat saying, "Hello, Tom, how's the family?" Gorman answered: "They died last night. Get in there and hit."

Mortality is a theme of Gorman's. He has a thousand stories about Durocher, with whom he had a difficult professional relationship, but for whom he retains affection. When Durocher had open-heart surgery a few years ago, Gorman called the hospital to ask how he was getting on. Later, Durocher called him back, deeply moved that Gorman had telephoned: "Gee, Tom, I can't get over you calling me. Of all people to call me . . . The trouble we've had. You've chased me out of so many games. The fights. The arguments. It's unbelievable . . . This really pleases me. Let me ask you something, Tom. Why did you call me?" Gorman answered: "Leo, I wanted to see if you were dying."

This story makes a rejoinder to an earlier one, from a time when both men were still active in the game. When Chub Feeney became president of the National League in 1970, he required all umpires on opening day "to shake hands with each manager and wish him luck." Gorman was umpiring a game that included a Durocher team, and he called Feeney to refuse the charge; Feeney said noncompliance would cost him three hundred dollars. Gorman breathed deeply, and at the appointed hour approached Durocher: "Hello, Leo, it's nice to see you. The best of luck for the rest of the season."

Durocher was adequate to the occasion. "Horseshit," he said.

In a mostly bad book called *The Yankees: The Four Fabulous Eras of Baseball's Most Famous Team* (it was from this book that I quoted

Murray Chass), Dave Anderson writes a good section on the Di-Maggio years. I remember Tom Boswell's story about DiMaggio, Marilyn Monroe, and the applause of crowds, and I love it when Anderson reveals once more the vanity of that noble horse: "Please pronounce the name the way he does. It's not Di-Magde-ee-o, it's Di-Mah-shee-o, as if he were an Italian nobleman." Anderson also recounts how DiMaggio, on a sweltering day in St. Louis, re-marked that he looked forward to playing a double-header. Some-body asked, "How can you enjoy playing a double-header in this heat?" The great man had a simple answer:

"Well, maybe somebody never saw me before."

Finally, there is the modestly titled *Number One* by Billy Martin and Peter Golenbock, which emphasizes dignity and character in all things. We find a Billy Martin baseball observers will recognize: combative, self-justified, vigorous, vulgar, shrewd, streetwise, self-pitying, and scandalous. Shakespeare might have invented him, as an inversion of Hotspur—a mock-heroic figure with Ancient Pistol's braggadocio and Falstaff's gregariousness. In *Number One*, the game becomes backdrop to the brash figure strutting be-fore it.

The book's major contribution is the portrait of Martin's ma-ternal lineage. He says of his mother's mother: "If you said some-thing she didn't like, she'd grab you by the hand and start biting you." He tells how his mother kicked his father out of the house when she was pregnant because she discovered that her husband was chipping on her with a fifteen-year-old high school girl. "To this day," Martin writes, "and she's older than eighty, she hasn't forgiven him. She told me, 'I'm going to outlive that son of a bitch, and when they bury him, I'm going to go to the funeral, and in front of all his friends and relatives, I'm going to pull up my dress and piss on his grave.'"

Two Poems

The Baseball Players

Against the bright
grass the white-knickered
players tense, seize,
and attend. A moment
ago, outfielders
and infielders adjusted
their clothing, glanced
at the sun and settled
forward, hands on knees;
the catcher twitched
a forefinger; the pitcher
walked back of the hill,
established his cap
and returned; the batter
rotated his bat
in a slow circle.

                But now
they pause: wary,
exact, suspended—
while abiding moonrise
lightens the angel

of the overgrown
garden, and Walter Blake
Adams, who died
at fourteen, waits
under the footbridge.

Couplet

Old-Timers' Day,
Fenway Park, 1 May 1982

When the tall puffy
figure wearing number
nine starts
late for the fly ball,
laboring forward
like a lame truckhorse
startled by a gartersnake,
—this old fellow
whose body we remember
as sleek and nervous
as a filly's—

and barely catches it
in his glove's
tip, we rise
and applaud weeping:
On a green field
we observe the ruin
of even the bravest
body, as Odysseus
wept to glimpse
among shades the shadow
of Achilles.

ET CETERA

Ace Teenage
Sportscribe

When I was a freshman at Hamden High School—in a suburb of New Haven, Connecticut—back in 1942, I became aware of a rakish character, a senior who wore chic jackets and loafers, who talked fast, and who aroused interest in glamorous seventeen-year-old women clutching books to their sprouting bosoms. I *think* his name was Herbie, and I *know* that he wrote about high school sports for the *New Haven Register*. I looked on him with the envy that I usually reserved for athletes. Herbie was no more an athlete than I was; writing newspaper sports was compensation for this bitter accident of nature. Gradually I realized that next year Herbie would be gone to the war, and his employers would need a replacement. I dropped some hints—and Herbie tried me out by allowing me to cover a couple of baseball games. I was hired. I met the *Register*'s sports editor—call him Ed McGuire—and signed on to cover Hamden High for ten cents a column inch. I was fifteen.

Autumn of my sophomore year was football and anguish. I rode the team bus to out-of-town games, the only ununiformed young male except for the manager who wore a leg brace from polio. I sat at the rear, behind already-shoulder-padded warriors like Batso Biscaglia the five-foot fullback, halfback Luigi Mertino, and Rafael

Domartino, the center who weighed two hundred and eighty pounds. At this time, Hamden was a colony of Calabria.

I sat at the rear in melancholy swooning isolation among cheerleaders in small green pleated skirts, little white socks, green sneakers—and great expanses of naked shimmering LEG. I sat in a lovesick impossible daydream, so near and yet so far—and the girls (the prettiest in school; by reputation the fastest) were pleasant and condescending. I heard them talk about dates after the game—each with her football player, one with a backfield—as they gossiped in front of me without taking account of me as *male*. Oh, I was male—and a hopeless shy devoted tongue-tied Oedipal nympholept, haggard and woe-begone, palely loitering on a bus to Ansonia. . . . The cold ride back from the game, which we usually lost, the players sat silent and hurt; the girls were quiet as they looked ahead to pleasing the sullen boys.

At home I would write a brief game story and my father would drive me down to the *Register* with it. Soon I wrote for the *Journal-Courier* as well, poorer and slimmer of the city's two newspapers, published in the morning while the *Register* came out in the afternoon. The *Journal-Courier* could not afford to pay ten cents an inch. Scottie MacDonald was Assistant Sports Editor (the entire staff) and promised me *lots* of by-lines and an occasional couple of bucks. I remember those offices in a second- or third-floor building in downtown New Haven. Scottie had a cubbyhole with a typewriter. He wore his hat all the time, set way back, above a brown suit and tie; he kept the tie pulled down and the top button of his shirt unbuttoned: pretty Bohemian for 1942. Every two or three weeks he handed me a slip of paper with which I could extract two dollars petty cash from the cashier.

I wrote my *Register* story first, then worked it a second way for the *Courier*. For the *Register* I clipped my columns, measured them with a ruler, and presented my column-inches to Ed McGuire, who wore a perpetual green eyeshade, who always looked angry, who tucked a continual cigar in the corner of his mouth. (Everybody entered the *Front Page* lookalike contest in those days.) He would re-measure my clips, take his cigar out of his mouth, spit, and write me a chit for the cashier. Eight dollars, maybe. . . .

I did not get rich as a sportswriter, but I observed an amelioration of my social life. To my astonishment, people like Batso began to wave at me in the cafeteria; Pongi Piscatelli, the famous tackle *six-feet-tall* smiled at me in the corridor and said, "Hi, John." Maybe he thought all Protestants were named John. Well, I thought, "Don" *sounds* a lot like "John."

Baseball was always my favorite sport and I liked writing about it; but neither newspaper printed much about high school baseball. Basketball was virtually ignored at Hamden High. Sometimes I covered games at our gym and watched as our midget centers and forwards planted their feet and pushed up two-handed set shots, often in the direction of the basket. We always lost thirty-eight to nineteen. When the games were away, or when they coincided with hockey games, one of the athletes would feed me box scores over the telephone and I would fabricate a thirty-word story to go with it. The three-quarter-inch gamestory would appear in the *Journal-Courier* under a by-line. Glory.

The glory and the glamor accrued to hockey. All over Hamden boys skated when they could toddle and played hockey as soon as they could lift a stick. Hamden was Ontario South. I do not know the etiology of this obsession, but it was a tradition; hockey was already king when my father was a boy, before Hamden built its own high school. The best neighborhood athletes concentrated their powers on hockey—which was difficult in those days, when there were few indoor rinks and only two or three months of good ice. Hamden's teams were good, and although the school was much smaller than its archrival Hillhouse in New Haven—Hillhouse beat us easily in other sports—in hockey we often prevailed. Hamden High's hockey players went on to play for Yale, for Harvard, for Providence College, even out west for Big Ten schools.

The biggest hockey occasions were Saturday night high school doubleheaders at the New Haven Arena, home of New Haven's minor league professional hockey team, site of Willie Pep's bouts as Featherweight Champion. West Haven, Hillhouse, Commerical, and Hamden gathered for hockey, and when the confrontation was between Hamden and Hillhouse, it was the Greeks and the Trojans. Often the crowd fights were as grand as fights on ice. Pongi Piscatelli, it was widely asserted, broke four noses one Saturday night alone.

The rule about no cheering from the press box was suspended for these games. There was a Hillhouse defense man I will call Bobby Adams who could not keep from smiling when his team was ahead. "Laughing-Boy Bobby Adams," I would write, "stopped giggling when Hamden's stalwarts forged three goals. . . ." Ed McGuire learned (from "Letters to the Editor," I suppose) that he had to keep an eye on my copy when Hamden played Hillhouse.

These Saturday night double-headers were my greatest challenge as infant-journalist because the *Register* turned into a morning paper on Sunday, and it was eleven at night before the games were over. I walked the few blocks from the Arena to the *Register* in wartime darkness and ascended to the deserted sports department, everybody gone home except an exasperated Ed McGuire. There he sat, cigar in mouth, eyes hidden under green celluloid, telling me I was late and everything was late for Christ's sake stop standing around get to work. . . .

The typewriter was an enormous old manual standard. I put a sheet of paper into the machine, spread out my notes, and began to type—one-finger . . . *Rapidly*, but one-finger . . . Ed McGuire sat at his desk half the room away from me and pulled from a pint bottle that he kept in a drawer. If I paused in my typing to think of a word—or to consider variant orthography; I could spell nothing in those days—his head snapped quickly up and he snarled something unintelligible except in import. Every now and then he stalked from his desk to mine, ripped out whatever I had typed, and disappeared to the Linotype room—presumably taking time to remove any "Laughing-Boy Bobby" editorials. I feathered another piece of paper into the steam-locomotive typewriter and continued midsentence.

That year was my career, for after sophomore year I transferred from Hamden to Exeter, where I found it impossible to get A's by literacy alone. Symptoms of Journalist's Swelled Head disappeared when my Exeter teacher gave me C-minuses on my first English papers: "paragraphs too short"; "newspaper jargon . . ."

Earlier, the swelled head had been temporarily helpful in the struggle to grow up. I cherished the *adventure*; I daydreamed myself Ace Teenage Sportscribe, and I noticed faint signs of interest from certain young women—not, of course, the cheerleaders, but girls who wrote features for the Hamden High School *Dial*, girls who read books—girls I could *talk* to.

In the dark *Register* building I finished my last lines for Ed McGuire, who took them to the Linotype room muttering imprecations. I put on my overcoat, mittens, and earmuffs; I stepped outside into the midnight air to wait a long time for the late-night bus that would take me four miles out Whitney Avenue and leave me at the corner of Ardmore to walk the dark block to my parents' house. I whistled white steam into the cold air of early morning, fifteen years old, thinking of *maybe* being brave enough to ask Patsy Luther to the movies—the proud author of a story right now multiplying itself into morning newsprint, ready to turn up on the doorstep in a few hours, large as life, BY DON HALL.

Rootcellar Fiveball

In one million basements, the green table with white lines and chipped edges, making for unfair bounces, wedges between the former coal bin and the tidy blue gas furnace. As I grew up, our cellar was like the other cellars, and I played my father when he came home from work, inviting him by snapping my fingers and flipping my wrist back and forth. Even when he came home tired and depressed from the office, which was much of the time, he played ping pong with me. At the beginning he always won, except when he threw me a game once a week or so. But I practiced. Between school and the time he came home, I wedged one half of the table top—the plywood had been sawed in half to get it down the bulkhead—against the ceiling beams and practiced against this backboard. By the time I was twelve, I was beating him most of the time. By the time I was fifteen and he was forty, I was beating him all the time, as he stood weary and hopeless by the blue gas furnace, his eyes failing and his head shaking. I threw him no games. He died of lung cancer just after his fifty-second birthday.

All the years of growing up—while I was a pushover in football, errant in baseball, earthbound in basketball, unankled in hockey—my wrist snapped a blue pebbled paddle against a light white ball and increasingly made the ball hit corners, drop over nets, spin unpredictably, scoot, bounce backwards. Long afternoons I practiced my weak backhand against the backboard until it was stronger than my forehand; then I built up my forehand again. I learned the footwork that shifts itself into the best place for the opponent's return. I learned not to slam but to change pace. I learned to vary placement, to spin up, spin down, spin left, spin right. I learned to slow the ball down, the way in any sport you achieve slow motion by long practice. Now if someone else's shot hit the table's edge, I could catch it on my paddle before it hit the floor and arc it up over the table end and over the net, so that it landed spinning the wrong way.

Other people in our suburb had ping pong tables in their cellars, and I played other adolescents from time to time. Mostly I won, even against better athletes, because I practiced more and because they did not take ping pong seriously. At camp, at prep school, in college I played ping pong, winning a low-key tournament once or twice. On the *Liberté* going to Europe, on the *Mauritania* coming back, going and coming across the Atlantic half a dozen times, I rose in tourist-class tournaments to the top, only to lose to some ringer who carried his own paddle with him.

In Ann Arbor, Michigan, where I settled down, I had no cellar big enough for a table. Therefore I played wearing leather-soled shoes in other people's cellars during cocktail parties, my necktie interfering with my backhand. Because I played seldom, I usually lost, at the start, a game or two . . . but seldom did I lose three games. The serve would come back first, then top spin, backhand undercut, forehand that would spin first one way and then another, and finally base-line placements. By the third game, I had learned the local handicaps that characterize gas-furnace pong: the forehand shortened by a two-by-four, the water-pipe hazard to a loop shot, the light that gets in your eyes when you go down for a low backhand, and the particular nicks of a particular table.

We would come upstairs sweaty, shirts out, sobered up, hair messed and faces flushed like teenagers returning from the drive-in; we would march to the bar for a drink, and my masculine superiority would swell to fill the mild suburban room. Ping pong was my twelve-point buck, my trophy case, my narwhal's tusk, my Saracen's skull from the Crusades.

One time a poet came to visit, from a wing of poetry different from my own; our factions had only recently declared truce after years of combat. We sat in my living room to talk politely but circumspectly. Conversation turned to sports. I learned that my guest had grown up a competitive tennis player, seeded in the South. Doubtless I must have introduced the subject of ping pong, and at once we became less circumspect. I supposed that I could handle him; he demurred with a gentle vehemence; I begged permission to disagree with polite but insuperable confidence; he found my confidence amusing if not touching in light of his own undeniable superiority; I found his conceit brash but delightful, humorous but pathetic, in view of my own eminence. . . . In short we played bragball with tireless, tiresome resourcefulness, but there was no table in my cellar at which to prove the point. We must have top-spun our boasting for twenty minutes before a bored observer finally suggested that we take our male validation down to the Michigan Union and rent a ping pong table.

Doubtless I would not be telling this story if it had ended otherwise: we played twenty-odd games; the visitor won the first nine by decreasing margins, and then I won thirteen or fourteen. A year or so later I read a poetry chronicle in which small but respectful attention was paid a book of mine—but, the author said, *can Hall play ping pong!* . . .

So I began to believe. My conquests in gas-furnace pong were monotonous. When I had not been beaten for a number of years, I decided it was time to emerge from the cellar. In the *Ann Arbor News* I read notices of the AATTA—table tennis, they called it in the association—and solicitations to sign up for league play in the gymnasium of Forsythe Junior High School. I telephoned the number and was asked if I would enter the league at the beginning or the intermediate level. I wanted to blush for them. Modesty forbade inquiry about the advanced, and, as I hesitated, the voice on the telephone suggested that, in case of doubt, beginning was recommended. I gave my name and agreed to show up on Monday night next, expecting to leap like the prodigy from first grade to graduate school.

Of course my comeuppance surprised me. Among the young beginning players I held my own, but I was clearly one of the beginning. We formed teams that played each other, sequences of singles and doubles each Monday evening. My first Monday I discovered that I held the ball incorrectly for service, not dropping it from the flat of my hand but clasping it between finger and thumb, a grip that could be used to impart spin to the ball before the paddle touched it. Several games passed before I felt easy with my serve.

But the greatest difference was space. In gas-furnace pong, there is always the coal bin and the two-by-four. At Forsythe Junior High School, our tables were far apart down the center of a gymnasium, allowing us movement backwards or sideways further than a ball could travel. At first this helped my game because my game was defensive. Wearing tennis shoes I could run back to catch a slam as it hoisted and slowed, then drive it deep to my opponent's corner, instead of relying entirely on a quick wrist. For years I had won by outlasting my foes, returning slams and good placements three or four times until in frustration the opponent slammed into the net or past the table's end. Now, with better opponents, I found myself returning five or six well-placed slams in a row, then a week or two later seven or eight of them. As we played week after week, my game may have improved a little, in placement and variety of spin, but it remained the same in kind. And my offensive opponents improved their accuracy. Now they could hit ten in a row, now twelve. Finally one slam would hit the net and drop over, or skip from the table's edge, while I was poised in center field twenty feet from the table. Or I would miss a return through fatigue. Then I skipped two Mondays in a row, flying away to do poetry readings, and when I returned the other beginners had improved so much that I was no longer their equal. It was the end of the term, and I did not sign up for another.

For ten years I played little. I bought one of those tiny tables you set up in the living room, on the rug, and store between times in a closet . . . but it was all restraint, all cuts and drops; I never took to it. Years passed—as the titles used to say at the movies. Middle age tormented me as it torments many of us. I was depressed; my life twisted and turned. . . .

After some years I quit my teaching job and moved to New Hampshire to write all day. It is a beautiful place to live, and my life turned beautiful, but it lacked the sporting side. My neighbors work with their hands, build houses, cut wood, and go hunting; I don't. Last summer we turned the old bedroom of our farm into the comfortable bathroom we lacked, and we built a new bedroom on the north side of the house. For heat's sake, we scooped the earth out underneath the new room, extending the old dirt-floored root-cellar—and opening out the space for a ping pong table.

I could not believe my luck. I ordered the best damned table that Sears and Roebuck sold, so constructed that it could rear up and form a backboard the way my father's table did by accident. This autumn I passed the day on which I became older than my father was when he died, and I passed it playing rootcellar pong, a suburban transplant to the country, playing with my wife.

Aware of the foolhardiness of wins and losses in a marriage, we play a game without points. We play rootcellar-fiveball-pong, keeping five or six balls in play—not, alas, at the same time, but in sequence—so that we need seldom stop to pick up the errant ball; when we do pause, we pick up the whole bunch. We are each other's hysterical backboards, furiously serving and returning, volleying a ball that would surely overshoot the table, hitting a ball on the second bounce or the slide if we must, keeping the air loose with a white ball flying. And if a ball pops up to the ceiling, zaps between two-by-fours, and drops on the table, we hit it again; if a crazy shot hits the cement block wall and veers toward one of us, we pretend we play squash and keep it in play. And when a ball is gone to the dirt floor one of us immediately serves another, so that our play is one long rally with a few ball-searching interruptions. In the heat of the moment, when a ball drops to the floor, sometimes each of us serves a new ball at the same time—and we work at doublepong for a few seconds at least. Continuousness is our game—which gives premium to new nonstandard techniques with the familiar props of paddle and ball: we flop on the table; we leap to volley . . . slam, cut, leap, scream, curse, serve, slam, cut, leap, scream, curse. . . .

In all the months we have banged the ball at each other for half an hour a day, we have never had a fight . . . .

BASKETBALL:

The Purest Sport
of Bodies

Professional basketball combines opposites—elegant gymnastics, ferocious ballet, gargantuan delicacy, colossal precision. . . . It is a continuous violent dream of levitating hulks. It is twist and turn, leap and fly, turn and counterturn, flick and respond, confront and evade. It is monstrous, or it would be monstrous if it were not witty.

These athletes show wit in their bodies. Watching their abrupt speed, their instant reversals of direction, I think of minnows in the pond—how the small schools slide swiftly in one direction, then reverse-flip and flash the opposite way. NBA players are quick as minnows, and with an adjustment for size great whales drive down the road. As a ball careens from a rim, huge bodies leap with legs outspread; then two high hands grasp the ball, propel it *instantly* down court to a sprinting guard, and *instantly* seven to ten enormous bodies spin and sprint on the wooden floor, pass, dribble, pass, pass, shoot—block or whoosh. . . .

Then the same bodies flip-flash back to the place they just departed from, fast as an LED display from a punched button—an intricate thrashing, a mercury-sudden pack of leviathans. . . .

In all sport, nothing requires more of a body than NBA basketball; nothing so much uses—and celebrates—bodily improvisation, invention, and imagination.

In football they measure forty-yard sprints. Nobody runs forty yards in basketball. Maybe you run the ninety-four feet of the court but more likely you sprint ten feet; then you stop, not on a dime, but on Miss Liberty's torch. In football you run over somebody's face.

When I was growing up, the winter sport was hockey. At high school, hundreds of us would stand outside at o degrees Fahrenheit beside a white rink puffing out white air, stamping our painful feet, our toes like frozen fishsticks. On the ice, unhelmeted shoulder-padded thick-socked blocky young men swept up and down, wedded to the moves of a black hard-rubber disk and crushing each other into boards, fighting, crashing, shooting, fighting again. Then we tromped home to unfreeze by the hot-water radiators, red-cheeked and exhausted with cold, exhilarated with pain and crowd-fight.

But basketball was a sweaty half-empty gym on a Friday afternoon, pale white legs clomping down court below billowing gym shorts; it was the two-handed set shot: pause, arch, aim, *grunt*. In the superheated dim gymnasium, twenty-seven friends and relatives watched the desultory to-and-fro of short, slow, awkward players who were eternally pulling up twelve feet from the basket to clatter a heavy brown beachball harmlessly off a white backboard. Always we lost thirty-eight to nineteen.

It was a hockey town, and New England was hockey country.

Meantime, elsewhere—in city parks, in crepuscular gymnasiums after school with the heat turned off, or in Indiana farmyards with a basket nailed to the side of a barn—other children practiced other motions . . . and the best of these motions found their showcase, over the decades and for decades ahead, in New England's metropolis, in the leaky old ship of Boston Garden.

When I was at college, I took the subway into Boston to watch college double-headers. My Harvard team was better than the high school I went to . . . but I do not recollect that we were invited to the NIT. I watched Harvard, Boston College, Boston University—and Holy Cross. Of course I remember the astonishment of one young man's innovations: the infant Robert Cousy, who played for Holy Cross, dribbled behind his back and passed with perfect swift accuracy in a direction opposite the place toward which he gazed. Or he faked a pass, put the ball to the floor, and cut past bewildered defenders for an easy and graceful layup. As far as I am concerned, it was Robert Cousy, and not Colonel Naismith, who invented basketball.

One of the extraordinary qualities of basketball is its suddenness of change, in pace and in momentum.

Years ago, when I lived in Michigan, I frequented Cobo Hall when the Detroit Pistons played there. I watched good players on bad teams: great Bob Lanier, Big-Foot with bad knees, enormous and delicate and always hurt; Dave Bing and Chris Ford, who ended their careers with the Celtics. Once I took my young son to see the Detroit Pistons play the Boston Celtics in a play-off game. It was 1968, the first time the poor Pistons made the play-offs. It was Bill Russell's next-to-last year as player-coach of the Celtics; they went on to beat the Lakers for the championship.

I sat with my boy and his friend David, who was a Celtics fan because he had lived in Boston until he was eight months old, and watched three periods of desultory play. There were good moments from Bing's Pistons, good moments from Havlicek and White—my man Cousy retired in 1963—but Bill Russell looked half asleep even as he blocked shots. In the fourth quarter the Pistons, astonishingly, led—and I entertained notions of an upset. . . .

Then my small charges developed a desire for hot dogs; I dashed out for a few minutes, and as I returned laden, I heard a swelling of wistful applause from the knowledgeable Cobo crowd. I looked toward the floor to see Bill Russell floating through the air to sink a basket. In the space of two hot dogs, Boston had gone up by ten points—or rather, not Boston but the usually inoffensive Russell. He had waked up—and when Russell opened his eyes it was over for Detroit. . . .

"Momentum" is a cliché of the football field, but it is a habit of the wooden floor. Basketball is a game not so much of important baskets or of special plays as of violent pendulum swings. One team or another is always on a run, like a madcap gambler throwing a dozen sevens. When the Celtics are down by a dozen points in the second quarter, looking listless, hapless, helpless, we know that suddenly they can become energized—rag dolls wired with springy, reactive power. We know that twelve points down can be six points up with a crazy suddenness.

Sometimes one player does it all by himself. On a night when Cedric Maxwell has twelve thumbs and Kevin McHale three knees, when every pass hits vacant air, when the foul-shooter clanks it off the rim, suddenly Larry Bird (usually it is Larry Bird) grows five inches taller and five seconds faster. With legs outspread he leaps above the rim to take a rebound, pivots, and throws a fastball the length of the court to Gerald Henderson who lays it up. Then as the Knicks (or the Bulls, or the Bullets . . .) go into their half-court offense, he appears to fall asleep. His slack jaw sags and he does his Idiot Thing . . . only to swoop around a guard and steal the ball cleanly, like plucking a sheep-tick off a big dog, then sprint down court and float a layup. Then he steals the inbound pass and, as the power-forward fouls him, falls heavily to the floor; only while he falls, he loops the ball up with his left hand over a high head into the basket—and *impossible* three-point play. Then he fast-breaks with Maxwell and Parish, zapping the ball back and forth, and leaps as if to shoot over an immense center. But, looking straight at the basket, he passes the ball blind to Robert Parish on his left, who stuffs it behind the center's head. . . .

We have just run off nine points.

This is a game you can study on television because it is small enough to fit in the box; and, through television's slow-motion replay, we study at our leisure the learned body's performances—as when Dr. J. or George Gervin soars from the base line, ball in the right hand, appears to shoot, pauses in midair, and, when a shot-blocker hovers beside him, transfers the ball to the left hand, twists the body, and stuffs the ball through the hoop.

It is only two points. If this were gymnastics or diving from the high board at the Olympics, it would be *ten* points.

The Celtics play team ball, passing, seeking the open man when defenders double-team Bird or Parish. The ball moves so rapidly, it is like a pinball machine in which the steel ball gathers speed as it bounces off springs, rioting up and out, down and across. Zany ball, with its own wild life, always like the rabbit seeking its hole.

> Or.
> The Game.
> Slows.
> Down.

Despite the twenty-four-second clock, there are passages of sheer stasis. The point guard bounces the ball: once, twice, three times. The guard in front of him is all alert nerves, arms spread and quivering. Will he drive right? Left?

> Bounce.
> Bounce . . .
> Bounce . . . . . .

He goes right NO-he-only-seemed-to-go-right-he-is-left-around-his-man, he rises into the *air* and . . . blocked-by-a-giant-under-hands-to-his-own-giant . . . who backward-stuffs it. BANG.

Oh, my. Basketball is the purest sport of bodies.

Kevin McHale,
For Example

═══════════════◈═══════════════

In the fifth game of the annual Celtics-Sixers play-offs, in 1981, Boston trailed in the third quarter, and Philly had just made a run. After the buzzer concluded a Celtics timeout, the weary green wandered back on court with that air of sleepiness under which NBA players disguise concentration. Referee Earl Strom held the ball against his chest and looked into the distance while Kevin McHale moseyed past. Suddenly, without looking in his direction, McHale flicked out a long arm and slapped the ball out of Strom's embrace—*stole the ball from the referee*—and dribbled rapidly toward the nearest bucket. Strom jumped, looked annoyed, and caught sight of McHale laughing—trailing in the fifth game of the play-offs, behind three games to one, playful as a boy. . . . Strom smiled—involuntarily, perhaps—as McHale threw him the ball.

Nine seconds later, of course, the two teams were again pounding each other into the parquet. The boys of the NBA, who mostly run from twenty-three to thirty-two years of age, play their games with a ferocity that would be grim if it were not boyish. Now Kevin McHale—boy-actor hair around boyish features, above an awkward-looking body—guards the lyrical Philadelphia forward Julius Erving. When Dr. J moves without the ball, McHale moves with him. When J pauses, McHale pauses also, fierce and solitary, staring like a cat into the blank unpopulated space between Erving and the ball, peripheral vision as alert as AWAC in order never to miss the ball as it is passed or Erving as he makes a sudden move. Then Dr. J has the ball and McHale hovers in front of him with his long arms cantilevered out from his sides, all of him trembling like an enormous hummingbird in his concentration, in his readiness to explode. J's face does its extraordinary imitation of catatonia—showing nothing, giving nothing, not an eye-flick nor a cheek-twitch—while the hidden computer of athletic intuition processes multiple data and flicks into action, looping and leaping . . . finger-roll . . . two points!

And a moment later, McHale blocks an Erving shot and re-bounds and outlets and follows up court to get the tap.

Then McHale fouls J; two for two.

Then J refuses to go for a fake; McHale fakes again; again the impassive genius of Dr. J stays put; the shot clock ticks; McHale looks to make a pass; everyone is covered. . . . So Kevin McHale falls backward, cocks his body like a trigger, jumps falling backward—and shoots over J's leaping forearm . . . two points!

For years we have heard talk contrasting playground basketball, one on one, and team basketball as played by the Boston Celtics. Celtic teams pass, run the break, and help out on defense, as all good teams must do. But any moral concentration on team basketball—on the stewardship and compassion of these enormous neighbors—overlooks the truth that team basketball includes and disciplines the skills of one on one. These educated individual bodies, one at a time, perform unimaginable feats of leaping and twisting. The five-bodied team flows like a school of minnows, and the seven-foot hummingbird darts delicately into the flower's heart.

It's practice that makes nearly perfect. The Celtics work out at Hellenic College in Brookline, Massachusetts, an institution that mostly trains young Greeks for priesthood in the Orthodox Church. Twelve athletes gather with three coaches, a trainer, public relations people, and a few reporters. At first the Celtics warm up slowly, stretching, rehearsing foul-shooting, practicing shots from different places on the floor. Cedric Maxwell faces the basket from twelve feet out—a shot that coach Bill Fitch wishes he would take more often—and sinks soft jumpers one after another. At an unoccupied basket Bob Ryan, who covers the Celtics for the *Boston Globe*, practices layups as if he daydreamed an unspeakable dream. K. C. Jones, elegant back-court man of Bill Russell's days, grayheaded now, strolls with a ball near another basket, dribbles twice, then bounces the ball hard, with English on it, so that it curls itself up over the rim and drops through without touching iron.

Now it is scrimmage time. Sitting at floor level a few feet from court's edge, you watch bodies and faces with a wonderful clear enlargement: Larry Bird, whose receding chin and slack jaw make him look dumb but whose bright eyes tell another story; Tiny Archibald with his compact, easy-flowing body, his face seraphic; Cedric Maxwell loping, so loose he might disassemble, skinny and muscular, alert and drowsy; and Kevin McHale of the strange construction, whom Bob Ryan sets in a tradition—the Funny-Body School of basketball players, like the Celtics' own Don Nelson, now coach of the Milwaukee Bucks.

It *is* a funny body. McHale hangs his long arms a little backward from his immense wide shoulders, pushing forward a chest enlarged by summer weight lifting, and in his pectoral development he resembles Margaret Dumont, the breasty virago of the old Marx Brothers films whom Groucho wooed so rudely. Coach Fitch, predicting that McHale will improve in the game, calls McHale's body immature, and then assumes the teasing tone endemic among athletes: "It's an incomplete body. He's waiting for the rest of the parts to come by mail." He sent away for them, Fitch adds, to *Mechanics Illustrated*. . . .

When McHale runs, he looks awkward. He lopes down the wood like an Irish setter, hair flapping like ears. In a 1982 play-off game with Washington, when the Celtics were down by five with twenty-six seconds left, McHale stole the ball and drove the length of the court to stuff it, dribbling and running with clumsy effective speed (and then taking over at both ends, rebounding, making a three-point play; the Celtics won the game in overtime). Danny Ainge told a reporter that McHale looked "like a baby deer on ice."

In scrimmage the play is hard, fast, often rough—and funny. These fellows are *competitive* sorts; if one of them changes from a green shirt to a white, his "Go white!" is as intense as his "Go green!" three seconds earlier. McHale cherishes nothing so much in the game of basketball as blocking a Maxwell shot, for they live next to each other, play cribbage, and drive to games together.

The Celtics are their own perfect adversaries, and they are also their own perfect audience. When Larry Bird swoops an unusual hook shot into the net, you hear a groundswell of approval noises. Then Rich Robey drives, stops, and shoots; Kevin leaps out of nowhere, invisible trampolines secreted in his size fifteen Nikes, to block the ball and tap it, like a volleyball, to Gerald Henderson, who breaks down the floor. . . . Applause is lighthearted but without irony.

Later the rookie guard Charles Bradley loses his balance going for Tiny Archibald's fake, and he falls into Tiny's body heavily—a palpable foul. But that relatively small, highly intelligent body— thirty-two years old, graduated from the University of Texas, El Paso, in 1970, twelve years in the NBA—does an extraordinary thing: as Tiny falls to the floor near the three-point line, his quick hands flip the basketball over Bradley's head and through the distant hoop. Everybody's jaw drops. There is a soughing sound, the mass exhalation of breath, noises of awe and envy, muttered *wow*'s, shaken heads, and smiles in the shaken faces.

Maybe Robert Parish is most admired and appreciated by his teammates, for his little flat jumper, for his exquisitely timed blocks, for his occasional guardlike seven-footer drives on the basket. . . . But the Celtics admire each other in general, and they let it show. Equally, they tease or ridicule each other for mistakes. When Cedric Maxwell blows a layup—almost turns it into an airball— the team *breaks up*, and for a moment everyone becomes hysterical including Cedric Maxwell; they slap their thighs, they roar, they clap their hands, they howl with abandon; and a moment later they hurl themselves through the air again, pursuing the ball, pursuing triumph at each other's expense.

At one point Kevin, leaping for a loose ball (like Tank McNamara diving after a fumble), cracks his elbow on the floor. He writhes in apparent agony. Bill Fitch looks not overly upset, and substitutes for Kevin, who goes to the sidelines and consults the trainer Ray Melchiorre. Kevin sits massaging his elbow in the sparse stands of Hellenic College, looking miserable, looking as if amputation were imminent. . . . Then Fitch, who has twelve players from whom to field two practice teams, brings the reluctant McHale back on the floor. A minute later he finds himself unguarded twenty-two feet from the basket, contracts his body (he does not flow to the basket; he snaps a spring at it) into a small jump and hits. The shot is beyond his range, and another rumor of approval murmurs itself from the floor, a noise that contains more amusement than awe. Then Coach Fitch's wry voice comments: "You'd better hit that elbow some more."

Like Auerbach before him, Bill Fitch motivates by sarcasm. Somebody asked him if it wasn't upsetting to the team that he would need to cut one member—either Charles Bradley or Terry Duerod—when M. L. Carr came off an injury. He answered that the players were glad it was not their decision. . . . Then his eyes lit up: he could *use* the tension. "Say Maxwell throws a pass at Charles Bradley, off his ankles instead of up around the numbers. I'll say, 'Hey, what are you trying to do, get Bradley cut? You put the ball up there where he can catch it and shoot it, maybe he will make this team, but if I let him go, don't forget, you were the guy who was throwing balls at his ankles.'" Fitch looks pleased with himself at this invention. "So, that makes a better player out of Maxwell."

They scrimmage an hour or so. Then the team gathers in a corner where Coach Fitch plays a video machine for them—back and forth, slow motion, stop-frame; he lectures learnedly on past errors and future problems, and concentrates especially on preparing for tomorrow night. Tomorrow the Celtics play Washington, and today's cartoon show illustrates Washington's endeavor in earlier games. Here the Celtics' response is good, here the Celtics' response is bad. TV time is a moment of repose after boisterous action, but Robert Parish concentrates mightily on words and pictures; so do Gerald Henderson and Chris Ford. Larry Bird looks as if his mind wanders, as if he had heard this before. Kevin McHale, his long arms clasped around his knees, rocks back and forth as he sits listening; he has always done well against Washington. . . .

After the illustrated lecture, a few players depart immediately for the locker room: Maxwell, Bird. . . . Others pick up stray basketballs and return to the court. McHale, still massaging his elbow, walks slowly to an unused basket and shoots by himself for twenty minutes. He pushes his little jumper, then he charges, and if his shot has missed he taps it in. Mostly his shots do not miss; he retrieves the ball, dribbles meditatively to another point on a semicircle twelve to fifteen feet from the basket, and sinks another. When he has missed from one place, he returns there and shoots again. He looks dreamy playing by himself—inward, pleasurably lost in the rhythm of habits, not so much the competitive extrovert as the introvert performing a solitary ritual.

Then Eric Fernsten approaches him and offers his services. Fernsten, in terms of minutes played, is twelfth man on the Celtics, and most of his minutes accumulate in the fourth period of runaway games. Mostly Fernsten is valuable at practice, where he plays the tall foe of the moment (Jabbar, Lanier, Malone, Jones) for the Chief to hammer on. And now he serves by guarding McHale while he whittles at the shape of his fall-away jumper. When no one fronts him, in solitary practice, he bounces straight up (a foot maybe; in a game he will jump higher) to spring his shot. When Ferny waves long arms in his face, McHale leaps while falling backward, gaining vision and distance, and loops a rainbow into the basket.

After a while they switch roles, so that McHale can practice shot-blocking, and he leaps to intercept the high arc—leaps and leaps, high off the floor of the Hellenic College gym, laughing and leaping, denying the fake and then falling for it, the two of them collapsing in laughter as Fernsten, when McHale is deceived into leaping, plays a six-foot-ten-inch guard, dribbles, and drives past him for a layup.

When Fernsten leaves, McHale practices by himself for ten minutes more.

When he emerges from the shower we sit in the stands and talk, McHale's long legs sprawled forward onto the court, his body draped over two rows of seats; every now and then he massages the wounded elbow. I ask him about playing by himself—the solitary practice I just watched.

"You mean like the stuff I do out here?" He leans forward to point at the basket. "The favorite times I have, the best times, are when I go into a gym by myself to play. . . . When I was younger . . . my father had two trouble lights and I'd hook them up, one in the gutter and one on the corner of the garage, to shine so that there would be a lighted court outside. I would play out there for hours, hours and hours by myself. . . . I used to go out there and play in the snow, shovel the driveway off, run in and my hands would be so chapped that I would warm them up on the radiator, go outside and play some more. The ball was cold, it wouldn't bounce, it was slippery, but. . . .

"I was *addicted* to the game. I would go into our high school gym in spring . . . everybody would be out doing track and I would just go in there and shoot and shoot and shoot for hours on end." He is amazed by the obsession of the fourteen-year-old, which has brought the twenty-four-year-old to the NBA. "The janitors all knew me; they would never *say* anything: they would just think I was crazy! I would go in there with my jump rope and my ball . . ."

"I have spent more time playing ball with myself than I have spent playing ball with other people. . . ."

When Pete Axthelm wrote *The City Game*—about the Rucker League, Earl Manigault, and NBA stars from the ghettos—he was, of course, accurate: basketball is *mostly* the city game. But as it happens, the central athlete of his book was a black man from the town of Bernice, Louisiana. Willis Reed's Bernice is smaller by 300 souls than French Lick, Indiana—population 2,000—where Larry Bird learned his tricks; and far smaller than the metropolis of Hibbing, Minnesota—population 16,000—where Kevin McHale worked on his solitary game winter and summer. By necessity, sportswriters covering professional teams live in big cities. Maybe they harbor citified notions of the unrelieved dullness of small towns—a dullness inconsistent with basketball street smarts. Surprising creatures come from quiet places—and the town of Hibbing has presented the world not only with Kevin McHale but also, a generation earlier, with Bob Zimmerman, whose family owned Zimmerman's Drugstore, and who is better known as Bob Dylan.

The American countryside is full of young solitaries, black and white; they shoot ten thousand foul shots in a row, or they practice chords, always accompanied by the internal music of imagined commentary. ("When I was in high school I daydreamed about the state tournament; when I got to college I would daydream about the Big Ten title or the NCAA. . . . This last summer I daydreamed Dr. J making different moves.") For all the gregariousness of the happy few, for all the wild speed and gymnastics, for all the IN-YOUR-FACE competitiveness of this game, there is a subjective basketball that peoples an empty gym with nine other players and thousands of spectators, and that keeps on playing when the lights are out and the body is asleep.

All over the world, for that matter, solitary adolescents practice greatness, especially in sport and in art. In Leningrad the twelve-year-old dancer practices on bare wood, two hours after the rest have gone home in the snow; in South Dakota the young man pulls himself from bed at four A.M., opens the deserted music building with his own key, and practices the piano until sunrise. And the chinless young fellow in Texas—not very strong, not very bright, covetous of fame—practices the rope trick a hundred thousand times. . . . Soon, he will join the rodeo; soon the small crowds of the Southwest will applaud in amazement at *his unfailing skill*.

Suitors of excellence, they are like Helen of Troy as the poet Yeats imagined her when she was young:

> . . . her feet
> Practice a tinker shuffle
> Picked up in a street,
> *Like a long-legged fly upon the stream*
> *Her mind moves upon silence.*

So athlete, artist, juggler, and courtesan practice their powers. Out of this drudgery and daydream comes the movement that wins the seventh game in the last seconds of the third overtime, or that plays Beethoven to a draw.

Kevin McHale was not heavily recruited for college. Hibbing is not known for basketball, and, although his high school numbers were good, college coaches doubted the opposition. But Jim Dutcher at the University of Minnesota knew what he saw—Kevin McHale arrived at Minneapolis in the autumn of 1977 to play with the likes of Mychal Thompson, and he quickly started and became All-American.

When the Celtics drafted him, third in the country in 1980, perhaps he was underrated again. In one of Red Auerbach's celebrated moves, the Celtics traded the first pick of the draft, acquired from Detroit, to Golden State for Robert Parish and Golden State's number-three pick—with which the Celtics chose McHale. For a time it looked as if number three would get away. As agent, McHale had chosen a Minneapolis attorney named Ron Simon, who was head of the University of Minnesota Alumni Association. ("I chose him because he didn't need it.") After the draft, Simon and McHale paid a quick visit to Boston, participated in a press conference—and then things went downhill. Mr. Auerbach and Mr. Simon disagreed on the issue of wages. McHale missed rookie camp, and in September he flew with Simon to the city of Milan in the fine country of Italy, there to discuss terms by which McHale would play basketball while undergoing European culture. Although both men claim that the trip was *sincere*, their investment in airline tickets turned out to be as profitable as $1000 invested in Polaroid in 1946. While they were negotiating with their hosts, Ron Simon made one last telephone call to Boston; on the transatlantic line, he heard a satisfactory offer, reportedly $320,000 a year for three years, hard.

When he flew back from Italy on September 8, McHale joined twenty other basketball players at Hellenic College. Bill Fitch, it was reported, did not wish to hear about jet lag. Nor did McHale complain that he had picked up, in Italy, a classic case of tourist's diarrhea. "I figured if I did, Coach Fitch would be on my case. He was mad enough at me. . . . I was *dehydrated*!" A year later, Fitch was still shaking his head. "He missed an awful lot." With evident pleasure he recalls McHale's diarrhea—"And he had hemorrhoids at the same time! . . . I saw McHale sitting in his own blood, with our stretching exercises. He wasn't about to ask me for more time off! I don't think anybody ever had a worse case than Kevin. . . ." He grins with the pleasures of *schadenfreude*—that invaluable Middle European concept: "the delight we take in the discomfiture of others."

Of course the NBA was a shock. First it was a shock because McHale had not expected much of it. "In college I thought the pro game was . . . a bunch of people making a lot of money who don't care what they do. But that's not true! Every team has great players! You work hard every night! . . . Boom-boom, cut-cut. . . . College ball is bounce-bounce, pass-pass, four corners. . . . It *can* be complicated, but sometimes it gets too complicated. Pro basketball is more exciting. . . . Hell, people say we don't dive on the ball. Throw the ball on the floor and see what happens! You can get your leg broken!

"You come in here and you get your ass whipped for the first three weeks. You think, 'Holy shit! What is going on in this league?' In college, a lot of times, you use your jumping ability and your size to jump over people and get the rebound. Here people are as big as you are. You've got to box them out, stay between them and the ball, use your body on them. . . . In college, I let the guy stand next to me and then I would outjump him. Here, you have to bump him and then go get the rebound. There is more *thinking* here."

Kevin Loughery, Atlanta coach, calls McHale one of the ten best players in the NBA; Jerry West calls him one of the best eight—and he cannot start for the Celtics. A *Sporting News* headline calls him the best sixth man in the game; *Sports Illustrated* features McHale in their account of this phenomenon, which has no parallel in other sports. The sixth man does not resemble a pinch hitter or a relief pitcher, is not used as a substitute for somebody having a bad day. In the volatile game of basketball, when passion switches its allegiance quicker than the Vicar of Bray, the sixth man is a designated emotional pickup—with the ability to go from nine to sixty in three seconds. No bullpen warm-up; no throwing on the sidelines.

For all his excellence, Kevin McHale cannot beat out Cedric Maxwell or Larry Bird or Robert Parish. The Celtics, you might say, are well off up front. As it happens, in an Auerbach coincidence, McHale is suited by temperament to the sixth man role; Bill Fitch claims that, even if he had him on a lesser team, "I still wouldn't necessarily start him . . . he's too valuable as he is. He can . . . go effectively from a dead start into a game that's already in motion."

Kevin McHale enters the game midway through the second quarter, urgently pulling up his pants, as if he expected them to sag to the parquet any moment. He looks both alert and relaxed. Like most athletes he trumpets unconcern: when he scored twenty-one points in his first play-off game, reporters asked him if he had been nervous: "The last deep thinking I did was my last history exam."

But nerves show as he twitches at his clothing on defense, waiting for his man to make a move. When Dawkins steps back out of range, McHale pulls down the shorts he had earlier lifted; they have worked up into his crotch. . . . Now Maurice Cheeks has the ball, Dr. J sets a pick, and McHale plucks at his jock strap, for all the world like a nervous child in kindergarten. . . . Will Cheeks go right? . . . Left? . . . He pulls up his pants again. . . . Right? . . . He twitches at his jock strap . . . Cheeks cuts around the pick, driving to his left, and McHale, helping out, leaps at the correct minisecond and covers the ball with his big right hand. When Bird rebounds, the tall men have suddenly gathered at the other end of the floor.

And when McHale commits a foul, he puts his hands on his hips and walks away from the criminal scene looking at the floor. . . . He controls anger; one cannot tell whether he is annoyed at the call or at himself. It is wonderful to see the best pros discipline feelings: the face remains impassive . . . and maybe if one takes care of the outside, the inside will take care of itself. The sensible athlete does not allow despair over one error to breed another.

After the game, it is all right to show feeling. The first time I met McHale—in the locker room after the two-point loss to Philadelphia in the first game of the 1981 play-offs—he came toweling out of the shower to his corner locker and crooned two syllables over and over, a melancholy ululation, a mantra of loss: "Oh shit . . . oh, shit . . . oh, shit . . . oh, shit . . . oh, shit . . ."

McHale's best friend on the team is Cedric Maxwell—sinuous forward from the University of North Carolina, Charlotte, rubber man, expert at squirming inside, scoring, and getting fouled. Kevin and Cedric live next to each other in a Brookline condominium a few minutes' walk from practice. They play backgammon—Cedric's chess is too good—and talk, talk, talk. . . . Besides talk they enjoy running games on each other. "Max is a guy you play practical jokes on. A couple days after Halloween, I had an extra pumpkin. A stairway comes down from upstairs right past a big window at Maxwell's place—you can look right into it—and on this window is a ledge. . . . Lynn and I carried a pumpkin there and I got a candle and we put it in his window. He walked down the stairs—and found that pumpkin looking at him! All he could see was the eyes!"

Perhaps in retaliation, Cedric Maxwell enjoys playing Cato, Inspector Clousseau's Korean houseboy, and will lie in wait to leap upon McHale—testing alertness, of course. Max will crawl into a dark corner, into a closet . . . and six foot nine inches of rubber man will leap out with an eldritch screech.

It was Cedric Maxwell who brought McHale *late* to his first NBA game: "I remember my first experience . . . Storrow Drive clogged up, horrible . . . Maxwell driving and Max is pretty easygoing. . . . We are supposed to be at the game like ten to six; Max picks me up at twenty to six—and I thought, 'I'm going to be late for my first day!' Max wasn't saying anything. . . . He was just eating a cheeseburger or something, McDonald's. . . . We didn't get there until twenty after six. Max just strolled in, and Coach Fitch just *shook his head*. . . ."

When I ask McHale where his height comes from, he tells me that the tallness genes are Croatian—his mother's side. (The name is all Irish, the height is all Croat.) I ask him how come, according to the team chart, he shrank from six foot eleven in his rookie year to six foot ten inches in his second year. Kevin answers without pause, "You shrink as you get older; when I'm done with this game I'll probably be a guard." For a moment we ponder the vision; then he goes on: "They just dropped me down. I am probably a legitimate six foot ten—Robert says he is a legitimate seven foot one. His *arms* make him a legitimate seven foot one." Thus I confirm that "legitimate" has special meaning in the NBA; it is used the way people use "literally" to mean "figuratively."

Then Kevin lurches a little to the side, reminded of the height that accounts for fame and fortune. He turns suddenly melancholy: "But it can be so lonely," he says.

This loneliness is a special type, afflicting only the famous—a loneliness deriving from the intimacy strangers try to force upon you. Of course, public recognition is unavoidable for basketball players. When you are a notorious offensive guard or a distinguished gymnast—not to mention a world-class violinist—you can often go unnoticed in public places, but their enormousness puts basketball players into a recognizable category. "You want to go out and have a beer or see a movie; you don't want to be hassled. . . ." You cannot stay alone or quiet, whatever your mood. Someone looms up with a huge smile, a pad and a pencil, hand extended for shaking. . . .

Every tall American, even some who find breathing strenuous, hears one observation endlessly repeated: "I bet you play basketball!" (People seem to think they have made a shrewd deduction.) Seven-footers develop answers: Artis Gilmore of the Chicago Bulls tells people no, he is employed by a zoo to wash giraffes' necks; McHale says no, he is a camel jockey—"I ride those camels round, you know. . . . Camel races, it's coming in. . . . You have to have long legs. . . ."

I ask him if the public hassling keeps him home. "I *refuse* to let this life make me stay at home! I go out, I go to Bruins games, I go to the theater . . . but it bums me out! . . . You hear people whispering your name. You think, 'Aw, Christ, not again . . .'" As we continue talking, the theme of notoriety through height returns. When I ask him about doing TV commercials, McHale worries: "You have to decide if you want just basketball fans to know you— or everybody." When he speaks with enthusiasm of Minnesota's governor from Hibbing, Rudi Pepich, I ask him if he has considered following Bill Bradley into politics. He says the notion is attractive . . . and then shakes his head; it would only move him from one public glare to another. When I ask a further question about height, he looks melancholy again. "Hey," he says, "people who are six foot ten don't think of themselves as being six foot ten *all* the time."

FOOTBALL:

The Goalposts
of Life

===================○===================

"Drop-kick me, Jesus"—entreats the country-western song—
"through the goalposts of life." As nearly as I can make out, from
dropping quarters into the juke at Blackwater Bill's, the song continues by enjoining the Son of Man to kick straight: "End over end,
neither t' the left nor the right." This anachronistic, deterministic,
masochistic conceit reveals the dynamics of fan and game as understood by the collective American unconscious. We watch from August into January—now, with the USFL, from March to July as
well—unable to ignore the game that pounds us in our armchairs a
hundred yards from end zone to end zone because without us no
game begins: for we are the ball.

Almost a decade ago I moved from Ann Arbor, Michigan, to an old
family place in New Hampshire. For something like seventeen au-
tumns I had attended football games at the University of Michigan's huge stadium. During my first many years, the Big Ten was
not the Big Two. Iowa was preeminent when I arrived in Ann
Arbor, and later Michigan State took its turn, but Michigan seldom prevailed. Coached first by Bennie Oosterbaan, then by Bump
Elliott, our teams were annually thumped by Ohio State, which

won the title more often than not. I remember Woody Hayes, leading by many touchdowns, restoring his first-string fullback with a few minutes left in the game—in order to hit the round number of fifty points. But I remember also miraculous 1964 when Bob Timberlake, quarterback who could run and place-kick as well as pass, took us past Ohio to the Rose Bowl where we beat Oregon State 34–7.

Things changed after Don Canham took over as athletic director in 1968. He had been track coach, a sport not usually associated with big money, and some of us assumed he would continue the relatively genteel tradition of Fritz Crisler: Michigan had held onto all-male cheerleaders, denying the networks their concentration on young female thighs; Michigan had featured football players who appeared to major in economics and minor in nobility of character. Instead, the new athletic director kicked Bump Elliott upstairs and hired Bo Schembechler to coach teams that WON GAMES, although their nobility quotient, like their literacy, might no longer stand scrutiny. Now the U. of M. athletic department advertised in the regional pages of *Time*, and the stadium filled every Saturday, more than a hundred thousand seats.

Heaven knows, I enjoyed myself, my last years in Ann Arbor, as the Maize and Blue regularly destroyed Northwestern, Wisconsin, Michigan State, Illinois, Minnesota. . . . Michigan became a power, annually ranked by magazines and wire services. Coed limbs scissored for the first time beside the yardmarkers in Ann Arbor. The halfback of the moment would run sixty yards at a clip, would score three and four touchdowns of a Saturday—until we played Ohio State, perhaps, or a nonconference wonder like Notre Dame, or until we lost in the Rose Bowl, outpassed, out-pass-defended when we tried to come from behind.

Most clear was the change not in team fortunes but in crowd. When I first attended games I sat in the end zone, in cheap seats available most Saturdays; only Ohio and Michigan State filled the stadium then. I would walk the mile from my house with my little boy and my friend Jim, among students carrying pennants and flasks. The male marching band would play, the male cheerleaders leapfrog, and the team fritter about, out of the single wing. No doubt students drank too much and passed out later in their fraternities, but the crowd of Ann Arbor people, swelled by alumni from nearby towns, was sober and traditional. There was little tailgating. As I sat in the end zone, young boys wandered on the wooden benches, half watching the game and half looking for mischief. The moment the whistle blew, they hurtled onto the field, throwing midget footballs at each other, falling down and rolling over, mimicking the ritual they had witnessed.

When promotion raised my salary, I bought three faculty season tickets, and my wife accompanied my son and me to the games. We sat low on the fifteen or twenty yard line among assistant professors letting go on weekends. We brought blankets to cover our knees, hand-me-down field glasses, and one of us carried knitting for the first half when the sun was warm. Outside the stadium we bought a half gallon of cider, and just before half time I ran out for three steamed hot dogs. Walking home we felt unusually tired, as if we had played hard, and we heard jazz blare from open windows and watched hearses and old fire engines hoot past us full of undergraduates: it could have been the twenties. Then, as likely as not, we would change our clothes and go to a cocktail party where we would talk with the other guests about the game everyone had seen.

It was all very collegiate. It is not much remembered that in this country football originated as the gentleman's sport; baseball belonged to the working classes. Football was like tennis, not bowling; it was like rugby, not soccer. The great New York Giant pitcher Christy Mathewson had attended college (Bucknell), like few ballplayers in his day. In *Pitching in a Pinch* (1912), acknowledging the social implications of his chosen profession, Mathewson referred to "those pompadoured young men with a megaphone . . . at a college football game." It makes me think of my two grandfathers, Mathewson's contemporaries, for whom the culture of weekends was inconceivable.

One was a farmhand's son who stopped school after the fifth grade, who delivered bulk milk as his father had done and then hired helpers until he became the owner of a dairy, a self-made businessman, a state senator, and a Republican boss. He lived to be ninety-one—proficient at reminiscence, hard and soft by turns, singer of old songs. He valued work above all things except health, and he valued health because it allowed for work. "Work, work, work," he recited with a resigned enthusiasm, pronouncing it in the manner of rural Connecticut and not just Brooklyn: "Woik, woik, woik." His one sport was riding horses, and it derived not from cutting a figure but from the workhorses he knew in his childhood. If he became too exalted to deliver milk, at least he could keep saddle horses in the dairy's stable and ride on Sunday mornings. He saw no sense in football. Let the pompadoured gentlemen down the road in New Haven, at Yale College, batter each other on Saturday afternoons.

My New Hampshire grandfather, son of a blacksmith, grew up with brothers playing baseball on a holiday—the sport of cut hayfields, of married men against single men on the Fourth of July, of games delayed by a ball lost in the stubble hay, games played without gloves, with bats turned on lathes in shops beside barns. This was the game that the troops played in the camps of the Civil War—my grandfather's father, black-bearded John Wells, played baseball while besieging Vicksburg—and that they brought home to the farm and the little towns, to play infrequently but with intense application. My New Hampshire grandfather loved this game, and he played catch with me beside the barn when he was in his sixties. He never saw a game of football.

In the 1920s—with the shorter work week, prosperity, broader schooling—preppy football became more proletarian. The colleges helped when they went semiprofessional by hiring steelworkers' sons from Pennsylvania. Now it was not so much the rich who bruised themselves, except in the Ivy League. But it was still a college game, whether played by the gentlemen or the players; and many of the players used the game for social climbing. Yale's captains still posed sitting on a wood fence without shoulder pads; it was the Frank Merriwell look, and it went with pompadours and megaphones.

My first experience with adults and football occurred early in the thirties, when I was about six. It remains one of those desponds of childhood that we carry inside us to the grave, perfect and miniature and damp with fresh tears. It was an appropriate introduction to the sport.

That year Yale played Dartmouth the Saturday afternoon of Halloween. My mother had basted me a ghost costume out of an old sheet, with holes for eyes and nose, which flowed over me like a snowdrift over a fireplug. The first house I went to was that of our next-door neighbors, the husband a Dartmouth alumnus. When I rang the bell and the door swung open, the rumble of drunk voices hurtled out into Spring Glen's evening, bellow and crash and whiskey smell. Aggressive friendly red smiling faces frightened me, blurred words shouted from stretched mouths. With a drink in one hand and a cigarette in the other, a man blew smoke through the three holes of my mask. Voices talking over each other pretended fear with false laughter. Then one young man knelt beside me, put his finger into an eyehole, lost his balance, fell against the wall, and ripped the sheet open across my face.

Although my parents took me to a drugstore where they bought the only mask still available—so that I became a ghost with the face of Mickey Mouse—I wept bitter tears. Although I gathered a bagful of candy from sober adults who perjured themselves by admiring my ghost-mouse costume, my memory of that night remains betrayal by the adulthood of colleges, parties, drunkenness, neckties, smiles, and football. Of course it was the world I was raised to join; I would go to college, as would the boys I played with.

When we played together, we imagined that we were college players, not professionals. I played touch and tackle with neighborhood boys in the back yards (bruised knees, torn knickers, runny noses, and the wonderful rasp of breathlessness) as we pretended that we were in the Yale Bowl. For me, college football was a radio game; tickets were expensive. I heard about games when

181

my parents returned from the Yale Bowl. They watched their little Bates College (Lewiston, Maine) upset the mighty Bulldogs of Yale in the Bowl by tying them 0–0, first game of the year in 1932. Once, while they watched Yale-Army, an Army player broke his neck and died making a flying tackle. I remember going to the Bowl a couple of times, and once somehow to a Harvard game; Yale won, and I walked off the field afterwards beside an enormous man wearing a Harvard uniform who was weeping large tears—I was astonished! Mostly I listened at home in the living room where the big Philco throated out the game. I remember the rich crowd noises from a few miles away, and the early gloom of November during the late, important games. One of the gasoline companies handed out free score cards for the games—it must have been a radio sponsor—on which one could record the plays. A straight line was a run, a wavering line a forward pass. Each time the ball changed hands you dropped the line lower on the blank space shaped like a football field, and your pencil took up a new direction.

Larry Kelly was a Yale end who caught passes, and he won the Heisman Trophy in 1936. Clint Frank won it in 1937—as if Yale had title to it—a single-wing halfback who ran and passed. When Frank was captain in his senior year, with no Larry Kelly to throw to, his team lost to Harvard; at the game's end, Yale substituted another passer, as Frank, who must have been the best athlete on the team, turned wide receiver—to no avail. Usually Yale beat Harvard, but I remember also the last game of 1941, when a tricky Harvard team—Harvard had a coach named Dick Harlow who was reputed to teach a complicated form of the game; sophomores could not handle it, but by the time his players were seniors they had the knack—starred a running back named Frannie Lee, who came from West Haven practically in sight of the Yale Bowl but betrayed the home folks by matriculating in Massachusetts. Harvard won 14–0, using fake reverses and a Frannie Lee forward pass.

Saturdays after Yale games were over, I spun the dial to find other games still playing, in the eastern middle west, and so it was that I first heard the female, grapy name of Ann Arbor. (Before the war, Michigan was in the Central time zone.) This staticky-sound-ing town was famous for football, and over the radio flickered the great name of Tommy Harmon, faint and wavering, distant and exotic, a Clint Frank pale with geography and wan with electric currents.

In the fifth grade we had our first football team. I cannot remember our coach's name; he was a neighborhood high school boy with a meaty face and an easy disposition. We practiced every day in somebody's back yard. It was before the revival of the T-formation, and a ten-year-old center snapped the ball back to something resembling a single wing. I played with the boys I had gone to first grade with—and second, third, fourth, now fifth. These were the boys from whom I would eventually separate myself in the wonderful alienation that began with reading books when I was twelve.

Of course, by fifth grade I was alien already, but I still thought it was my fault rather than my glory. My father worried about it more than I did, for I was an only child who played alone a lot, and when I found a friend, we usually quarreled after a few days. I stood a little to one side in any group, more full of wist than of scorn, a little shy, possibly afraid, possibly bullied. . . . It must have occurred to my father that I might be a sissy. Doubtless he bought me the football uniform in order to help me be a regular fellow. And doubtless, because I was the only boy with a football uniform, it underlined my difference. But at first it did what it was supposed to do. My ten-year-old playmates looked on me with awe, as I wore my faintly padded khaki knickers, my blue jersey with Clint Frank's number, and my blue and silver thin-leather helmet. I became instant team leader; I became fullback; just before we played our first game, which was also our last game, I was elected captain.

Two miles away was another grammar school the same size as ours, Putnam Avenue School in Whitneyville, where my father had done his eight years. We played their fifth-grade team in an empty lot on a Saturday morning in October. Captain and fullback, I had reached the height of my athletic career; I could not run, or pass, or catch, or block, or tackle. Putnam Avenue won. I recall only one play of that morning in detail—though I can recollect the feel of everything: the taste of dirt, the cool wind, the sore lungs and scraped legs; humiliation, ineptitude, fear. . . . When I tried to punt, one time, I dropped the ball so that it hit my knee not my foot, and the ball clunked backwards over my head.

In the sixth grade I became a substitute lineman; I played one play against Putnam Avenue. In the seventh grade I did not make the cut. In the eighth grade I discovered literature, in the ninth I wrote poems. . . .

I continued to follow the game. I watched Hamden High play on Friday and flipped the radio dial on Saturday. On Sundays I listened to the Brooklyn Dodgers professional football team because they shared Ebbets Field with the team of Whitlow Wyatt and Peewee Reese. Thus I was listening when the announcer interrupted the play-by-play to tell us that Japanese aircraft were bombing American positions in Hawaii. I called upstairs to my napping parents; had they heard? . . . They had heard, and my father made plans to be drafted; and I imagined flying something like a Spad over something like trenches. . . .

As it happened, my father was too old and I too young. In 1942 I left Spring Glen Grammar School for Hamden High, where football, like boxing and obstacle courses, was patriotic because it prepared us for combat. Boys I cheered for, making tackles and bruising themselves on frozen Connecticut dirt, died on Pacific beaches less than a year later. . . . But football was not fashionable at my high school, which was hockey crazy and sent hockey stars to Yale, to Wisconsin, to Providence College. When Johnson's Pond froze over in winter, neighborhood boys swept snow off the ice and spent their afternoons playing pickup hockey games. Hamden's baseball teams were poor, its basketball horrible—five-foot-two-inch Calabrians missing set shots—and its football disappointing. Our athletes were tough and strong but they were not large. (There was even something *wrong* with being large. I remember a gym class where a boy hurt his foot and took his socks off to reveal toenails an inch long. When the gym teacher gently asked him why he did not cut his toenails, the boy said that if you cut your toenails it made you grow tall.) I remember our fullback, Batso Biscaglia, who was over five feet tall, composed of oblong slabs of muscle—two parallel chunks thick from ankle to thigh, a double chunk forming the trunk, a short oblong the neck and head. I remember a stylish halfback named Luigi Merdino, skinny and quick, who collapsed when touched; I remember an end, Gino Fuscolo, whose chunky red face turned blue on exhausted November Friday afternoons.

After two years of Hamden High, I was translated to Phillips Exeter Academy, where we lost to Andover even when we brought in ringers in 1946. In earlier years our players had names like Wentworth and Potts—I mean their first names—but in 1946 we had a roster of boys named Bob, Timmy, and Jim. *That* was the year we were going to beat them, after the humiliating 28–7 loss of 1945. Even our bench swarmed with veterans, ex-Marines of advanced ages like twenty-two, and at least two quick halfbacks. Well, an Andover man ran back the opening kickoff, and they kicked the point after; we pushed them around all afternoon, scored only one touchdown, missed the extra point, and lost 7–6.

Then I attended Harvard. From my freshman year on, when Robert Kennedy played end and Ken O'Donnell was quarterback, we lost and lost and lost. We lost to Dartmouth, whose student body then vomited for eighteen hours in Harvard Square. We lost to Yale, three years out of four. My friends on the team became doctors, one a psychoanalyst. One year our captain was a linebacker who played the violin, maybe the best hundred-and-thirty pound linebacker on the whole East Coast. . . . The night before the Yale game, excited by the occasion if not by Harvard's prospects, I was banging around Winthrop House with some friends when I came upon our captain, uncharacteristically drunk, ricocheting from wall to wall. The next day he played quite well. . . .

Of course I was ignorant. If I knew that Harvard was bad because it lost, I had no idea how bad our opponents were. When the team flew west in 1949 to play Stanford, a friend who played tackle told me that the team needed two planes to fly out but would only require one for the return: they could stack the bodies. Stanford beat Harvard 44–0, and the schools agreed to cancel the reciprocal game scheduled for the following year. When I saw my tackle-friend he was on crutches. I asked him what happened. "Howie fell on my leg," he told me. Howard Houston was captain that year.

I spent one year at Stanford, a couple of years after graduating from Harvard. All students, even people on fellowships to write poems, got to watch the game free. Each Saturday I arrived early to watch warm-ups. I enjoyed the wonderful solitude a stranger finds mingling with a crowd in a new place: a warm California Saturday afternoon, beautiful cheerleaders, the crowd frivolous and good-natured, ironic like Harvard but lighter. . . . Of course, the football was not so light.

One of the best linemen, a guard with no neck, lived on the back road that curled from our flat to the campus; often I picked him up hitchhiking: he was friendly, inarticulate, gentle, dumb. In his dumbness he did not resemble most of the Stanford squad, which was brilliant and sloppy by turn, uniformly devoted to the forward pass. The next year John Brodie would arrive and Stanford football would improve—but my year there was good enough for me: we fielded a senior quarterback named Bobby Garrett, All-American, who later played for the Cleveland Browns, and a receiver named Sam Morley. They played an astonishing game. After a spell of penalties, on fourth down and thirty-five yards to go, they would not punt; they would complete a long pass. You never knew what would happen next: the team was asleep, the team woke up; they looked like Harvard, they looked like . . . the New York Giants!

When I returned to Harvard the next year, to be a Junior Fellow for three years, I never attended a game. Then, at Michigan, I caught up with football again. Because most of my classes took place in the afternoon, I rarely taught athletes, who practiced or worked out all year. But in my first years I taught mornings and thus made acquaintance with a halfback named Bert Martin in a course called "An Introduction to Poetry"; twenty-eight or thirty students came together for a fourteen-week term and I tried to convince them of the beauty, pleasure, and discipline of verse. Bert asked me about the course before enrolling; he was nervous to talk with me, anxious to take the course, even more anxious to do well. He came to my office many times that term: polite, formal, diligent, conscientious, and concerned to improve his grade. Was I being operated on? Eventually, I decided that Bert was straight as an arrow— because he showed me some poems he had written. He was a big, shy, blond boy who blushed easily. When he showed me his poems, the scene was as corny as an Andy Hardy movie; he almost broke his neck making sure that no one watched from the hall; he guarded the door as I went over his poems. They were love poems, and they were not very good, but they were no worse than the poems of most students I taught. Because we shared a secret, we became closer. We were able to talk with each other about poetry, football, life. . . .

His papers improved, I suppose because he was out of the closet, but when he answered essay questions in class, he was terrible. Although he wrote A papers, and wrote them himself, I had trouble giving him a B in the course because his exams were dreadful; Bert failed under pressure. I remember watching with dismay his big muscular pink body knotted over a little desk, the pen lost in his fist while sweat rolled from his forehead on a cool morning. He shook, his brow furrowed, his foot tapped rapidly on the linoleum, his neck twisted, and I could see his eyes roll. He would write a word or two . . . stop, cross out . . . write a little more, crumple the paper he had started, begin another. . . . In the end he would hand me half a page.

And he was consistent, as he showed one autumn Saturday. It had been a wretched season for Michigan football; we had lost to Michigan State, to Minnesota, to Wisconsin; we entered the final game gross underdogs to Ohio State and playing at Columbus. Miraculously, we kept close to Ohio, and going into the last few minutes we were behind only 0–7. Then we began inexorably to march down the field, running the ball, with Bert doing most of the running. Four yards. Seven yards. Three yards. Eleven yards. I listened on radio, cheering not only my team but my student. With seconds left to play, we were on Ohio's goal line and it was Bert who was chosen to carry it in, and who ended his football career—tense as he was at a midterm—by fumbling the ball just before he leapt into the Ohio end zone.

If University of Michigan football was mediocre when I arrived in Ann Arbor, the Detroit Lions enjoyed a heyday. Bobby Layne was still there in 1957, and it was the year they played Cleveland for the championship of the NFL. Tobin Rote took over when Layne was injured, and the Lions won 59–14.

For many years thereafter, the Lions were strong, with great defense, but lacked the offensive resourcefulness to become champions. But there were offensive moments: I watched on television the famous 1960 game at Baltimore. When Johnny Unitas threw a pass to give Baltimore the victory—apparently—over Detroit with fourteen seconds left, millions of fans around Detroit turned off their sets; after they read the papers the next morning, they never turned off a game again until the gun sounded—for, after a four-second kickoff, Earl Morrall threw a pass down the middle to his slowest receiver, Jim Gibbons (Baltimore defended against fast receivers at the sidelines) who ran untouched over the goal line as the game ended.

Each year I liked the pro game better; therefore I squatted at dead center of the male American psyche, which found itself, as the sixties started, increasingly drawn to violent Sunday afternoons. This was before Sunday double-headers, before Monday Night Football with Howard Cosell, before the Special Thursday Night Edition of Sunday Night Football with Howard Cosell. . . . I picked up Lions tickets when I could. Season tickets still accounted for most good seats at Tiger Stadium, but I could get decent seats for exhibition games and occasionally for regular season games with unfashionable opponents. My son and I would sit together, watching Alex Karras sack a quarterback and Yale Lary run an interception down the sidelines; watching Jon Gordy pull from his guard position to lead an end sweep for Hopalong Cassady, watching Nick Pietrosante struggle up the middle, and Dave Middleton and Gail Cogdill leap to catch touchdown passes.

Bill Veeck put it down to the malaise of a decade: "The sixties was the time for grunts and screams. Football passed baseball." My favorite game began to seem old-fashioned, slow, dowdy. . . . In football the shocks were greater, there was more trickery; in one game the San Francisco 49ers, with John Brodie at quarterback, surprised the Lions with a lineup that resembled the old single-wing short punt formation (it is called the shotgun now) for which the Lions were unable to improvise defense. The underdog 49ers rolled over the Lions. . . . Seven days later the secret was known and defenses discovered.

As usual when I was interested in something, I decided to write about it. I wrote to public relations at the Detroit Lions Football Club, received some sort of roster—nothing worthy of being called a press kit—and met a PR man lately recruited from the *Detroit Free Press*. I attended practice at Cranbrook, took note of Milt Plum's powder blue Bermudas and Earl Morrall's khaki shorts, watched drill, studied scrimmage, and eavesdropped. I heard Nick Pietrosante ruminating on soap operas—what is happening now in *As the World Turns?*—and glimpsed the off-season habits of professional football players. I hung on the edges of things along with other middle-aged men and crowds of boys. I watched Earl Wilson and Bill McPeak coaching. One morning I watched the Olympic hurdler Glenn Davis, world record holder in the 440, practice pass patterns. "He *gains* speed when he *cuts*," said a defensive back named Bruce Mahar. That afternoon Davis fell, separated a shoulder, and was finished.

I watched the offensive guard Harley Sewell, bald and helmet-less in shorts and jersey, rehearsing in July heat the moves he had practiced so many summers as a college player and as a professional: lining up facing an imaginary defensive line, he assumes a three-point stance and glares ahead; at the crack of a *hut*, his aging body uncoils in a spasm of energy, he pulls, runs fiercely across the line, and cuts upfield to take his angle on a linebacker.

It was the first time I had observed professional athletic training, the process of learning game parts before assembling them into whole games. I was dazzled. When I tried to write about the Lions, the prose came out dazzled. I cannot remember whom my agent showed it to; the last magazine to turn it down was *Boy's Life*.

These were the early sixties, when John Fitzgerald Kennedy played touch football on the White House lawn, before assassinations, before the commitment of American troops to Viet Nam. Something inside ourselves and our country wanted grunts and screams. Although in my asinine article I noted fashion details like Milt Plum's hairdo—Earl Morrall and the troops wore crew cuts; Plum's businessman's hair stayed combed after hours of practice—it was largely the hurtling of huge bodies like Roger Brown's that I attended to. Although I praised the elegance of enormousness, I used verbs like *smash*; I spoke of *bruise, hurt, force, sprain*.

Late in the sixties my wife and I separated and divorced. On Saturday afternoons in the autumn, I took my son and daughter to Michigan games, and, because I wanted occasions for closeness with my son, I bought season tickets to the Detroit Lions. By this time the Lions had been mediocre for several seasons, and seats were easier to come by. We sat high in the grandstand on the twenty yard line, third-base side of the field. We had three seats, and on Thanksgiving Day my daughter came with us. Otherwise there was a series of small boys, one of my son's teachers, occasional friends of my own. . . . We kept the seats for five years, until the season when I gave tickets away more often than I went.

Disaffection came gradually. For a long time my son and I each pretended to like it more than we did. Finally we understood: we were partly repelled and wholly bored. If once we saw something unusual—Lem Barney as punt returner appears to let the ball stop among down-field opponents, then darts between them, picks it up, and runs top speed down the field for a touchdown—if once we saw inventive panache, ten thousand times we saw the "run to establish the pass," and "the passing situation" varied by the draw. . . . If once we saw some athletic ingenuity and spirit, five times we saw a big young man, padded into anonymity, writhing on the ground in pain with a torn knee that would keep him out of action for the rest of the season—and that would, if he lived to be sixty despite the cardiovascular damage of steroids and amphetamines, leave him crippled and walking with canes or crutches. . . . We watched as powerful youth faded in one violent moment to crippled age.

And Chuck Hughes died on the field. He died from a heart so bad that he would have died anyway, even if he had kept to his bed. So the papers told us. (In our decades of public mendacity, one would have to be psychically crippled to read any institutional claim of blamelessness without doubt. . . .) Whatever the etiology of his disease, his death was appropriate to the scene and its feelings, for the crowd was vicious. The crowd loved not only the blood but the man-to-man action that made the bleeding. If it resembled the fight crowd more than the car racing crowd, the violence was of course more random: the people at a fight love the single boxer whose muscular near-nude body they appraise. But the hulks on the football field lack human characteristics and reveal their identity only by numbers and labels. Their identity is the color of their jerseys. They assault in groups: gang tackling is at the center of football, as the confrontation of two people, pitcher and batter, lives at baseball's center.

It was not the players or the game that turned repellent; it was the drunk, angry, male crowd. We often came early for parking's sake and to watch practice—more handsome than the game, when things happen with the perfection of dream: the long pass arcs for sixty yards hitting the wide receiver in full stride toward the goal line; the punt travels eighty yards in air with a hang-time of an hour and a half; the field-goal kicker rides his kick sixty-seven yards splitting the goalposts (of life) as one might split a beer. . . .

As we sat enchanted by dreamlike skills, the crowd gathered around us. Behind us a young man in a bright blue windbreaker wore a zombie mask and was toking a joint through his mouth hole. Others arrived at twelve-thirty P.M. on a Sunday, staggering drunk, arguing drunkenly over tickets and seats, counseled by grumpy old ushers who occasionally resorted to policemen. I came to loathe a group of seven or eight men in their forties who sat eight rows in front of us. They wore sweaters over their neckties, they brought whiskey, they shouted that everybody sucked. . . . These were *the boys*, the masculine fraternity I turned away from in adolescence. *What was I doing here?* One man in particular sticks in the mind. He was lean and sinuous, wore a brown suit, and his face was meaty with liquor. At some point, by the fourth quarter, he would rise and go through a little act in which he played a homosexual, or what he fancied as homosexual. He flipped limp wrists, his lean hips swung bumping and grinding, he leaned his head sideways, rolled his eyes, and shouted in falsetto, "*Thay now!*" Oh the self-mockery of secret desire! The man's companions, every Sunday, roared obligatory laughter at his obligatory seizure.

When the crowd for the Michigan games changed, it was not that a new athletic director changed something into his own image; the age demanded its own athletic director. As pro football emerged from the television set—bloodying the carpet, eating everything in the refrigerator, leaving beer cans on the piano top—Saturday afternoons took on the look of Sunday afternoons. The crowds were not identical—more women went to the college game, and more families, so that the Michigan crowd was more gentle than the crowd at the Lions—but it became a football crowd rather than a college crowd. Subway alumni, they used to call the street fans. These were station-wagon alumni, prosperous couples from Birmingham and Pontiac, Dearborn, Bloomfield Hills, Grosse Pointe and the other Grosses; from the small towns outside Ann Arbor—Milan, Saline, Manchester, Chelsea; from Toldeo, disloyal to distant Ohio State; from Flint, desperate with ugliness and tedium. All morning the Buicks and Chevrolets, the Oldsmobiles, Pontiacs, and Mercurys, the Lincolns and Cadillacs parked in the lots near the stadium, big cars driven not by the men who made them but by lawyers who represented auto companies in workmen's compensation suits, managers who set production goals, and advertisers who dreamed up desires, coloring the hair blond and the teeth white. There were the big bosses and the little bosses, the doctors who treated the ulcers and detoxified the alcoholics, morticians who buried the rich earning riches as they embalmed, owners of grocery stores and package stores, sheriffs and judges, mayors and deputy mayors, dentists who straightened the teeth of bosses' children, who filled the cavities caused by the braces, who performed the root canals and the gingivectomies and punished the middle age of the middle managers sitting beside them in the stadium.

The two crowds were aspects of the same, distorted by class difference, for the men at Tiger Stadium were line workers and the Michigan couples white collar middle class. Which is to say that the Ann Arbor bunch had more money and averaged 2.2 more years of education. . . . But the differences converged toward a new center. Now the Lions crowd had boats and RVs; and the Michigan fans were never the spoiled pompadoured patricians Christy Mathewson mocked, but the bewildered and enraged managers of a moribund culture. The classes melded together, unconscious of convergence, in the hobby of violence—by which I mean not an idea of violence, please, but murder, rape, suicide, blood, broken bones showing splinters through skin, entrails on the sidewalk, lips swollen, and cheekbones dislocated so that not only is the face unrecognizable but it is also unrecognizable as a face; as well as violence after the crime: nightmare, phobia, sweat, psychosis, exploitation. It is a violence economic, political, social, and historical, pertaining to These States, which I, loyal to These States, wished not to see.

But it is not only violence, or simple violence. It is an organized and socially endorsed mob ritual of licensed fury, unrelated to winning games, and used as a letting go of intolerable feelings that mount and gather increasingly in the mass heart. It is violence flattered by the rhetoric of a sniggering crunch-porn in the sports magazines: "The Worst Enforcers in the NHL," "Bad-d-d Dudes in the Pivot," "He Throws at Your Head with All His Heart," and "They Call Him Crippler."

It is a fury we cannot detach from an underclass the game exploits. It is suicidal fury, exhausting itself in taking blows. *And we are the ball.*

Just before I left my teaching job at Michigan, I taught another football player, the first after Bert. This young man played for Bo Schembechler when the University of Michigan was beating or tying Ohio State for the Big Ten title every year. The class was freshman English, a one-term exercise in composition. The student I call Darryl Bott, who now plays in the NFL, was handsome, tall, energetic, amusing, fresh, charming, hip, streetwise, bright, and incorrigible. When he attended the first meeting of the class, he sat in the front row, the only black student. (Typical of the University of Michigan, the class resembled a patrol from a World War II movie: one black, one Chicano, one Oriental, two Jews; several students from small towns and countryside, several more from Detroit, three or four WASP suburbanites; a born-again Christian whose essays proselytized his teacher, four Catholics, a high-jumper on a track scholarship, two nurses. . . .) Darryl stood out, and not only for the color of his skin. That first brief class, when I required self-introductions, he let us know that he had arrived, much recruited, to play for the Michigan football team. When I had the class write a brief impromptu, I discovered that his talents went beyond the football field; he could write an English sentence—easily a B with work, maybe better.

When the class met the second time, he arrived twenty minutes late; my annoyance vanished in the quick deference of his apology, and in the warm smile he flashed us all. Then I did not see him for two weeks, when he arrived half an hour late for class. He said he would talk with me after class, and wrote that day's impromptu on the subject of visualizing football plays in daydream in order to anticipate and rehearse situations that would occur in real games. Again he wrote decently, and as I read his paper I felt encouraged, for in our conversation he told me with considerable emotion about his mother's illness back home, his necessary absences to take care of her, and his resolve to attend class henceforth without fail, and, of course, to make up the missed work. After all, he confessed, he had chosen Michigan over the other university suitors because of its academic standing; he mentioned law school. . . .

He never came to class again. Ten days later I was conferring with a boy from the class and mentioned my worry over Darryl's disappearance. The boy shook his head and smiled, the way you smile about someone gifted to get away with everything. Yeah, the student told me, he teased Darryl about it every afternoon when they scrimmaged on the basketball court. . . . Discovering that Darryl was not kneeling at his mother's bedside, along with my irritation I felt worry. Of course I could not give him a grade if he did not do the work, no matter how many passes he intercepted.

When I gave him his E, the telephone began ringing. Academic counselors from the athletic department—joshing, friendly voices —worked on middle-class professional guilt over race, youth, naiveté, poverty; ambition, promise, failure, disgrace. Would I not, the voices urged, let the boy do the work?

No.

More voices, and then Darryl himself. One rainy Sunday morning in June, he walked to my house bareheaded, soaking wet, and sat in my living room. He was not smiling now. He told me that if he flunked out of school his mother would have a heart attack and die. He told me he would do anything to make up. When I said he could do nothing to make up because he had missed classwork with other students, he sat for a long time on the sofa without speaking, then walked away in the rain.

The phone continued to ring; voices turned unpleasant. One day a professor telephoned from an academic board within Michigan's College of Literature, Science, and the Arts—"LS&A," the liberal arts college within the university. He gave me support; Darryl had taken E's in all his courses, and the athletic people were ridiculous, trying to reinstate him for the fall term. I was relieved to hear that there were four E's and not just one. Still, I felt bad for Darryl; I was sure that his false expectations were not entirely his own doing; he had been led to think that he could get away with anything. Secure in my knowledge that he couldn't, I even felt bad for the football team, when I read in the papers that Michigan would field a young and untested defense this autumn, but that sophomore Darryl Bott was expected to star. . . .

That was the summer I left Ann Arbor for New Hampshire.

When the fall schedule came out, I discovered that the first national football game on TV included Michigan. I watched in astonishment as Darryl Bott, student-athlete with four E's, played a competent game.

When I wrote to the LS&A professor who had telephoned me, I found out how this trick had been taken. In July or August, Darryl Bott had been admitted to the School of Education retroactive to January when he first came to my class. (Most eminent football players enroll in Schools of Education, separate from liberal arts colleges, where they take courses in football science toward degrees in physical education.) A graduate student in English assigned Darryl five papers and gave him a retroactive B in freshman English. At the same time, because no one is allowed to drop out of LS&A with unfinished courses, it turned out that Darryl had never been enrolled. None of his records were to be found, and therefore, obviously, he had never enrolled in my class at all. . . .

There went Darryl's law school. There went the B.A. Like most student-athletes who play football and basketball at big-time schools, Darryl never took a degree. I know it is a story endlessly repeated. But Darryl *could* have gone to law school, or learned to use his brain, if he had not been exploited. He thought he could rip us off; we know who got ripped off in the end, don't we? . . . to serve the audience gathered on Saturdays, a hundred thousand at a time, drinking martinis at the tailgate, screaming for victory, driving back to their policed suburban compounds, with car doors locked lest black people assault them at stoplights. . . .

East was the country of rocky fields and fourth-rate college athletics. That October, shortly after I watched Darryl on television, we drove up to Hanover to see Harvard beat Dartmouth. My delight in victory was tempered by my astonishment—returning to the Ivy League after seventeen years of the Big Ten—at the athletic ineptitude of many players. Not all of them—almost every year somebody from the Ivy League made it to the pros; there were people named Shula and Kemp on that Dartmouth squad—but most were hysterically bad, doubtless future country-club golf and tennis champions, but not ATHLETES. There were defensive hulks as ponderous as tortoises and twice as slow; there were wide receivers who placed one foot in front of another while footballs fluttered out of reach; there were fat guards daydreaming at the ball's snap, pushed on their rumps by thin wide-awake linemen, who slept later. These teams executed plays the way blind men with Parkinson's disease executed horses.

On the whole, I enjoyed the game.

Virtue is not a product of athletic incompetence. Perhaps these teams are throwbacks to amateur days and serve thereby to enforce Ivy League self-esteem, but the old days of the pompadoured young men were not of themselves virtuous. (People of Darryl Bott's shading were not invited to play.) Certainly the crowd in Hanover seemed anachronistic, carrying flasks in the floppy pockets of muskrat coats. But most of us, that Saturday, only weekended in the past—tourists in an athletic Stockbridge. Come Monday we would return to the city of corporate greed, and at night bed down in the suburbs of vacancy and violence—Harvard and Michigan together, Detroit, Boston, and Hanover.

Of course, football's violence, new or old, is gentleness itself compared to the interrogation rooms of Lubianka Prison, or to any street in El Salvador. . . . As I grow older, John Calvin's or John Milton's view of man's nature seems more appropriate than Thomas Jefferson's. The Roman Empire that Gibbon describes, with crucified slaves bordering roadsides like poplars in France, seems normal in man's history; anything more gentle is a momentary deviation. When the inmates of a New Mexico prison, freed by rebellion for a few hours, employed their freedom to gang-rape, torture, and kill each other, I suspect that they revealed Natural Man. If this be so, the new football crowd makes Michigan Stadium a soft Coliseum; but it was not the vision of man's nature entertained by the Enlightenment forefathers. . . .

If we need reminding of social difference and historical change, we can look at the logo of the New England Patriots, the professional team down the street. The logo features a young man in colonial costume, kneeling as a lineman under a tricorn hat in a three-point stance. *But the face!* It does not resemble the paintings of James Montgomery Flagg, or earlier paintings of Minutemen. . . . Instead, this Patriot repeats the hulking face of a superhero in a comic book—thick-necked, leering with mayhem, giggling with sadism, brow furrowed not by thoughts of his tiny dinosaur-brain but by anabolic steroids—an image of the decline of the Republic's hero from enlightenment ectomorph, spiritual with endeavor and guilt, to sadistic, hulking, mesomorph, and apelike Homo Footballus, the object of our weekend attention and obsession, squatting before the goalposts of a diminished life.

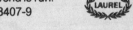